"The advice and guidance from the many returned sister missionaries in *Tell Me about It, Sister!* was so valuable for me as a woman and mother, and I didn't even serve a mission! I felt uplifted, inspired, and anxious to continue the essential work of missionary service in my daily life. This book isn't just for returned missionaries; it's for also for women who want to add daily inspiration in their lives."

 —STEPHANIE NIELSON, author of *Heaven is Here* and the blog *The Nie Nie Dialogues*

"Andrea provides a refreshing and helpful perspective for any returned sister missionary! *Tell Me about It, Sister!* cleverly puts into words the feelings you are having, normalizes your experiences, and inspires you to move forward with confidence and excitement. Each chapter provokes you to explore, process, and better cope with the journey of coming home. Her witty and insightful literary approach will leave you laughing, empathizing, and invigorated. This book is the perfect companion as you adjust to this final transfer of coming home!"

 —BRITTANY COLTON, returned sister missionary, Tempe Arizona Mission; Child and Family Therapist LGSW, Bethesda, Maryland

"We all go through periods of adjustment—no matter who we are. Returning home from a mission can be a time of wonder, a time of hardship, and everything in between. This book is a fabulous help—it is full of gentle and thoughtful reminders to keeping the spirit during the transition. It is laced with humor, wit, and charming and sincere personal anecdotes, and it will be a huge blessing to every sister who reads it. Every time I pick it up I am uplifted, renewed, and enlightened on how to apply the lessons from my mission in my current life. This is a must-read for every sister—whether she is a freshly returned missionary of twelve days or twelve years."

 —MELANIE BURK, returned sister missionary, Brazil Rebeirao Preto Mission; owner of Fifth and Hazel Design, San Diego, California

"When I first read this book, I'd been home from my mission for several years. I was impressed at how relevant and beneficial it still was. It was just what I needed to recalibrate myself with the woman I had become on my mission. Though I grew in leaps and bounds while serving, I came home unsure of what to keep and what to leave behind. Years later, immersed in marriage, kids, a career, and callings, I envied the testimony and perspective I had back then. *Tell Me about It, Sister!* was the perfect guide to redirect my thoughts and habits to become the friend, wife, mom, and member missionary I knew I could be.

"This book gives practical advice and inspiration to all returned sister missionaries, married or single, young or old, struggling or succeeding. It is a one-of-a-kind look into how we as returned sisters missionaries can carry our skills and strengths to wherever we are 'called to serve' next."

—ANDREA POND, returned sister missionary, Illinois, Nauvoo Mission; Nationally Certified ASL Interpreter (NIC)

TELL ME ⬇
ABOUT
IT, Sister!

A GUIDE FOR RETURNED
SISTER *missionaries*

TELL ME ABOUT IT, Sister!

A GUIDE FOR RETURNED SISTER missionaries

ANDREA FAULKNER WILLIAMS

CFI
AN IMPRINT OF CEDAR FORT, INC.
SPRINGVILLE, UTAH

ISBN 13: 978-1-4621-1650-8

Published by CFI, an imprint of Cedar Fort, Inc.
2373 W. 700 S., Springville, UT 84663
Distributed by Cedar Fort, Inc., www.cedarfort.com

Library of Congress Control Number: 2014959318

Cover design by Shawnda T. Craig
Cover design © 2015 Lyle Mortimer
Edited and typeset by Emily S. Chambers

Printed in the United States of America

10 9 8 7 6 5 4 3 2 1

Printed on acid-free paper

Dedication

To my boyfriend, Brian Todd. Thank you for always being willing to listen to just one more mission story.

To my mama. Thank you for setting the supreme example of how a returned sister missionary should act.

To Jo and Walker T. Thank you for taking such long naps so your mom could write this book.

Contents

FOREWORD
by C. Jane Kendrick

O N THE NIGHT I CAME HOME FROM MY MISSION, there was no one at the airport holding up signs or balloons or drooling babies I had never met. I remember there was a janitor, the buzzing of his floor cleaner, and the shine of his waxy pathway up the terminal. Behind me were my parents and two sisters who had flown to Montreal to pick me up at the mission president's home. But the rest of my family and friends were forty-five minutes away in Provo, surely asleep since it was a dark, late night/early morning in October 1999.

We had missed a flight in New York, certainly due to our lazy driving tour of the northeast coast. We had bouillabaisse in Maine, cream puffs in Boston, and traffic from New York City to JFK. When our plane left without us due west to Salt Lake, I remember my mother being upset. But I was relieved; I was nervous about experiencing that epic missionary moment of getting off the plane into a whooping, hollering crowd of my excited tribe of origin. I loved my loved ones, but slipping back into Utah in the black of night relieved me of that too-intense spotlight.

After eighteen months of emotional and laborious religious work, I was tired. Fatigued. Bedraggled and homely. During a worldwide missionary training, I had heard Elder Jeffrey R. Holland preach about committing wholly to the work. He said, "Go home on a stretcher. Impress the deacons." I didn't come off that airplane on a stretcher, but I came home a wobbling, tipsy, weary spirit with many inches of dark roots on my head, pasty skin, and an internal image of me belly crawling to the finish line. And even though I had loved learning to preach the gospel in French, my throat often hurt from creating sounds and shaping words I had never used before.

So, what happened next? Well, I don't remember much, perhaps because I slept a lot. Coming home felt like a birth of sorts; I was sensitive to everything ("This song on the radio is *so* wicked!"), and I had to learn many new tasks—like "checking my email" and "surfing the web" and accepting a new me. I really was like a newborn, or an alien, or a robot turning into a real human. It was the most surreal time of my life. Things felt weird; flirting or wearing pants, for example, felt like sinful indulgences.

But after a while I decided I needed to adapt. I cut my long hair and colored it blonde—signifying a new identity I suppose. I let my mother buy me new clothes, even though I fought the feeling of vanity when we shopped for much bigger sizes than the ones I wore before my mission. I dated my former district leader (you say you'll *never* do it, but you do), and I enrolled back in college. Little by little I discovered who I was without yellow, crunchy day planners and a supportive—if not sometimes annoying—companion by my side.

What I didn't have, you now do: a guide on how to traverse that great divide between your missionary identity and your post-mission self. What I would've given for the tips and ideas you now have in the pages of this book! Subjects range from dating to depression, including tips on how to write about your new reality and face it using the same skills you learned as a missionary. Because you are holding this book in your hands right now, you're far better off than I was fifteen years ago.

With one caveat: fifteen years ago, skinny jeans had not yet been invented. I cannot imagine the shock of wrangling myself into a pair so freshly off my mission in an attempt to feel "normal." But this book even includes ideas on how to handle that one.

Welcome Home!

C. Jane Kendrick is a writer, blogger, columnist, and community activist. For eight years she has cultivated her award-winning blog CJaneKendrick.com where she writes about life, religion, birthing, wifehood, motherhood, womanhood, body acceptance, her love of community, and all the spaces in between. For the past four years, she's worked on Provo's most exciting cultural event, The Rooftop Concert Series as founder, coproducer, and host. She's also written for the Deseret News, The Arizona Republic, *and* Segullah, *and has published a book of her essays called* C. Jane Enjoy It! *In 2011, Mayor John Curtis crowned C. Jane Queen of Provo with a tiara and tears. But to her family, she's Courtney, wife to Christopher Kendrick, and mother of four.*

HEY, SIS! IT'S ME!

Called to Serve

AS A JUNIOR AT BYU, I WAS THRILLED TO BE RECEIVing my mission call. I had taken years of Spanish and could just envision myself in Chacos and a linen skirt in a remote village in the Andes. I was sure I was South American missionary material! So, naturally, you can imagine my surprise when I was called to the Illinois Nauvoo Mission to serve in the visitors' center. I'll admit, at first it was hard to accept the idea that I would occasionally be wearing a pioneer dress. (Okay, I'll admit it: I broke down and cried about that.) *But* I quickly felt confirmation that this was where I was called to serve. I spent the first six months of my mission in Nauvoo and then received a separate call to proselyte in the Colorado Colorado Springs Mission—in Spanish! I was delighted to serve as Hermana Faulkner, and after six and a half months in Colorado, I returned to Nauvoo to finish my mission.

I loved being a sister missionary. I loved the long days in the visitors' center, knocking doors, spending hours on my knees with my companion, shedding tears over investigators, and working with members. As a missionary, I had difficult days, lonely nights, and more exhausting mornings than I can count. But overall, I was happy because I had a great purpose as a servant of the Lord.

Reconciling the Old with the New

Then all of a sudden, it was over. To my surprise, the transition home from my mission was far more challenging than I had anticipated. I returned to college, moved in with a wonderful group of returned missionary roommates, and saw the people I had served with often. I felt like I came home a better person who had a deeper love for the Lord and

1

for the world in general. Aside from a fear of small dogs (I was chased by a lot of Chihuahuas in trailer parks!), I came home feeling more at peace with myself and looked forward to the life ahead of me. Teaching at the Missionary Training Center enabled me to spend an additional eighteen months preparing elders and sisters for their missions. As an added bonus, within the week I returned, I met my to-be husband. We dated, we got engaged, and exactly a year after my return home, we were married. I had an incredible support system. But, even with all of this, most of the time I felt like I didn't know who I was or what I was doing. I had come home from my mission optimistic and with so much enthusiasm for the next chapter of my life. How could someone with so much direction and support feel so lost?

Why do so many of us feel lost when returning home from a mission? I have considered this question time and time again and have concluded that there are two parts to coming home from a mission. The first is a physical reconciliation with your old life. This involves taking off your nametag; putting on your old clothes; and returning back to a schedule of school, work, dating, callings, and friends. This is not always as simple as it sounds. (For one thing, the old clothes might no longer fit!) The second is a spiritual reconciliation. This involves taking the new "returned sister missionary" you and incorporating her into your new life. It requires incorporating the principles you learned on your mission—principles that changed your heart forever—into your everyday habits. This spiritual reconciliation is the more challenging of the two. It might take a few weeks or even months to feel physically home from your mission, maybe longer. But the challenge of *spiritually* uniting your mission self with your former self will take much more time. This is a good thing: It is a challenge worth praying about, fighting for, and investing time in because this unification is how to truly bring your mission home and continue to be blessed by it forever.

What Will You Find in This Guide?

This book will serve as a guide as you make the transition home from missionary service. Again, when I refer to coming home, I am referring not to the few weeks of physical adjustment but to the implementation of spiritual principles learned on your mission. Use this book to measure your progress as you continue growing spiritually after returning home from your mission.

To get a broad perspective on this complicated issue, I have enlisted the aid of over two hundred returned sister missionaries. Many were interviewed in person, and the rest were contacted on the phone, in surveys, and through email. These women were asked to talk about the challenges they faced in the years following their missions and how they found success. I was humbled by their stories, and I am excited to share them with you. I read these stories over and over, overwhelmed by the wisdom that was shared. My husband would often walk in and find me huddled over my laptop, crying as I read the story, advice, or challenges of yet another amazing woman. These are shared throughout the book. In addition, I have included a few interviews with a special group I call "Superstar Sisters." These women have mastered the principles we are talking about in this book, and each offers a unique perspective. I hope that reading the experiences of other sister missionaries will remind you again and again that you are loved, that you are not alone, and that you are a total rock star. It is the truth!

You will also find self-analysis quizzes at the end of many chapters, modeled after the attribute quizzes in chapter 6 of *Preach My Gospel*. These quizzes are intended for you to use over and over again as you analyze your progression. Throughout the book you will also find journal prompts, where you can record your thoughts and experiences. Finally, I have included reading suggestions: books, scriptures, and articles that have guided many of us in our paths as we have sought to grow and find our place in the world. But I hope that, more than anything else, you will find in this guide a reminder of God's love for you.

Girls Only! No Boys Allowed

I would like to mention why this guide was specifically written for sister missionaries. "The Family: A Proclamation to the World" teaches us that, "Gender is an essential characteristic of our individual . . . and eternal identity and purpose." We were created as females before coming to earth with spirits that were intended to nurture and care for those around us. This sensitive, nurturing predisposition is what makes us women and is an attribute we should cultivate and develop; it is a blessing to have this sensitivity. It is one of the reasons that we are wonderful missionaries who touched lives in different ways than our male counterparts. With the blessing of sensitivity, however, also comes a natural resistance to being uprooted. For sensitive souls, transition and change can be exhausting, even wrenching!

Over the years I have watched as roommates, friends, and the sisters I served with have come home from their missions. Growing up, I listened to the stories of my own mother as she shared memories of post-mission ups and downs. Many sisters come home and experience the highs and lows of transition for weeks, months, and—in some cases—years. Were these sisters doing anything wrong? No! They were just being girls! And interestingly, although sisters experience myriad emotions returning from their missions, not one of the sisters I interviewed said they regretted serving a mission or would change their transition home in any way.

In addition, until very recently, sister missionaries in the Church have been more of the exception than the rule. While sister missionaries are out serving, most of their female friends and siblings are pursuing marriage, school, and careers. Returning to school and singles wards often leaves sisters feeling out of touch. With the recent announcement of the change in age requirements for service, we will see more and more sisters serve missions and at younger ages. But that doesn't change the fact that because fewer women than men serve missions, it often feels like there isn't as clearly of a defined place for returned sister missionaries. We are still a minority in Mormon culture.

The decision to serve a mission in no way makes us better or advances us above any other women in the Church, but it does place us in a unique situation, not only in the mission field but upon returning. For that reason, I decided to create something I wish I had been given: a book of advice, reflection, and anecdotes that we can refer to together as we continue to grow and mature as returned sister missionaries. The journey home from a mission is beautiful and difficult at the same time. A journey like this is meant to be shared. So, sister, I think we should take this trip together. You in, girlfriend?

Chapter One

OVERCOMING PHYSICAL CULTURE SHOCK

"When we left on our missions, we were told to leave everything behind and to lose ourselves in the work. I believe that when we return home, we are to do the same thing. We need to leave mission life behind us (not the lessons we learned or how it changed us—just the lifestyle) and jump with both feet into the next part of our lives. If you do that and give it your all, whether in dating and marriage or school or a job or a combination of those, the Lord will bless and help you achieve all you can. He wants you to have success as an RM just as much as He wanted you to have success as a missionary. Don't waste time being awkward or wishing you were back on your mission."
—Sister Felicia C.

HI! WELCOME HOME, SIS! REMEMBER WHEN YOU served a mission? That was really great! But you're home now, and it is going to be really great too. I remember the day my oldest brother returned home from serving in Novisibirsk, Russia. His mission was deep in Siberia, a place I thought was somewhere people only joked about. He had an eventful mission filled with things like shopping at stores run by mobs and tracting in forty-below weather. While he was away, my parents built a new home. After his fifty-two hours of travel and grand welcoming at the airport, we drove directly home. We couldn't wait to walk him through the new home and show him all of the upgrades. After he spent two freezing cold years in a dark, lonesome part of the world I am sure this San Diego Tuscan-style villa was a harsh contrast. I still remember looking up at my brother while we walked around and thinking he had changed. I saw in his face what an amazing two years he had experienced and how shocking his return back to "normal" life must be.

At first, coming home might seem challenging and overwhelming. It might be a culture shock. But with time you will come to see how much your mission has blessed your life. This chapter describes situations that you will face upon arrival home. When I arrived home, there was a feeling of displacement that I now realize was a good thing. It came as a direct result of following the counsel I had received from the prophet in my mission call: "You will also be expected to devote all your time and attention to serving the Lord, leaving behind all other personal affairs."[1]

When I was a missionary, I prayed and prayed to do things like "forget myself and go to work" or to "focus." Feeling out of place for a period of time when I returned meant that I had been successful in following this counsel. We must have been such great missionaries, right? And we are going to be great returned sister missionaries, I promise! Below I have identified five elements of "culture shock" you might encounter upon arrival home.

1. Finding a New Lifestyle

> "It is really important to have both feet at home again after your mission. It was an important and crucial part of your life, but you can find confidence that you did everything you could as a missionary as you look at your future with an eye of faith and hope. Your future is as bright as your faith." —Sister Kimberly W.

Some people recommend coming home and jumping right back into school; not wasting a week, day, or minute to allow yourself to get discouraged. The question is, what will be the best thing for your life? I had originally planned on coming home and starting school midway through the semester on the "block" schedule. A week after returning home, I realized how happy I was to be at home reacquainting myself with my family and life, and I decided to change my plans. Instead of rushing into the next phase, I took a break. I enjoyed being home with my parents, visited my siblings, started dating again, spent time finding a job, and even took a nap or two! The month I took "off" was so wonderful. I learned a lot about who I was and was able to process the marvelous experience I had as a missionary. I didn't regret it.

When you come home, allow yourself time to be still and to heal from any challenges you faced while serving, mentally or physically. If keeping yourself busy like you were as a missionary is what will keep you happiest, then dive right in. But if you come home and feel like a break would be nice and there is an opportunity to take a breather, take it. You've earned it.

2. Focusing on Yourself

> "My biggest challenge was transitioning from focusing on the gospel and other people full time to spending time studying, working, and dealing with 'real life.' It makes it harder to feel and recognize the Spirit because you have to focus on so many things. It helps when I have meaningful Church callings that help me focus on things of the Spirit." —Sister Keri N.

For most missionaries, one of the most challenging parts of returning home is turning your focus from thinking primarily about others to thinking primarily about yourself. The attention you need to give the little things like school, work, and life's logistics can be really exhausting.

Renewing your driver's license, grocery shopping, and apartment hunting might feel empty and pointless, but those mundane daily tasks are all necessary. You might feel discouraged that your time socializing with family and friends, working, or going to school is not allowing you to study the way you did on your mission. Rather than being discouraged about not being able to maintain the missionary schedule, find a way to schedule in study and prayer, service, and opportunities to fulfill your calling in a way that works and will allow you to be successful.

Tell Me about It, SISTER

GG When I first came home, I spent time trying to figure out how I could become a missionary again. [My mission] was an experience that gave me a purpose; I knew I was doing the right thing, and I was close to the Spirit. As a missionary, you are always thinking of other people, and you really put yourself last; but when you come home, that completely switches. Everything you do is suddenly all about you! Do you go to college? What is your major? What will you do with your life? Who are you? What do you like to do? Who do you date? How do you date? It was extremely difficult for me to go from spending sixteen hours a day thinking about saving humanity to thinking 'only' of myself. It felt wrong. All of the sudden, I felt like I needed the Spirit more than ever, but I wasn't able to focus on doing the things that breed the Spirit like I could as a missionary. That was really hard to accept." —Sister Katie H.

3. Creating a Schedule

6:30 a.m. wake up, 7:00 a.m. exercise, 9:00 a.m. personal study . . . Well, now what am I supposed to do with my time?

The schedule for missionaries is created around the one purpose they have been given, namely, helping others come to Christ. It is an amazing feeling to fill in those fifteen-minute time slots in your white planner with this one goal in mind. As an RSM you have multiple purposes, and your schedule will require some diversity and flexibility. This switch from a singular purpose and focus in life can be confusing, but it in no way means your life should lack purpose or structure.

It will be smart for you to maintain many of the habits you acquired as a missionary, especially the habit of organizing your time. Structure is a beautiful thing. Here's what Mandi says about maintaining a schedule after a mission:

"I wasn't embarrassed about still keeping a detailed calendar, because I remembered to plan days and times off where I would be the one to organize social events with friends. That got me right back into informal social scenes, meeting new people, and dating." —Sister Mandi B.

At first it may be difficult to find a balance between maintaining good habits and allowing a little flexibility for social and family events to move into your schedule. With time, this will become easier, especially as you turn to the Lord to ask Him how He wants you to use your time.

4. Finding a New Line of Work

My dad has a saying he often repeats: "Don't worry if your works are hard and your rewards are few; remember the mighty oak was once a nut like you." Sometimes we are working hard and it doesn't feel like we are getting anywhere. But one day, we will look back and think, "Oh, that's what it was for. I have really become something." Right, Dad? Work hard at whatever you do. At first you might not feel the same satisfaction you felt from the activities you were involved in as a missionary, but you can have faith in the fact that you are working hard and progressing.

I like how Julia described this:

"When you come home, you enter a new stage of life where you need to dedicate time to the Lord for spiritual growth, but doing things like going to school, working for your future, making friends, and dating should also be considered activities dedicated to the Lord. You're fulfilling other areas of your life that are pleasing to Him. So even though I wasn't spending all day studying and teaching the gospel, I still felt the Spirit when I was trying to do my best in all areas of my life." —Sister Julia M.

I love that! She still felt the Spirit because she was *trying* to do her best in all areas of her life. That is all the Lord expects of us.

5. Taking Time to Readjust

When I asked a couple of hundred sisters what they wished they had known coming home, they all said: It takes time! In one way or another, almost all of the people surveyed mentioned that time is the most necessary resource to rely on when coming home from your mission. I think that when looking back, these sisters realized that time was what helped them most in their transition home. But how do you do that? How do you give yourself time while moving forward with the rest of your life? Let's take a look at a few examples of sisters who found successful ways to transition to their home lives while granting themselves time to adjust.

"I kept in contact with other returned missionaries from my mission, and I slowly transitioned away from my daily planner (I brought home a few extra) and kept trying to follow the same study schedule. I also prayed a lot and tried to keep myself as busy as possible with member missionary work. Basically, I tried to put myself through my own MTC for reentering the world." —Sister Nicole M.

An MTC for reentering the world? So wonderful! After I had my first baby, my sister-in-law wrote me a beautiful email about giving myself a fourth trimester. She said we should give ourselves at least three months after our babies come to accept our new lives and not worry about getting in our jeans or being right where we thought we would be. What if you gave yourself twelve weeks after your mission to learn to be you again—wouldn't it be nice to have that time set aside? What if you need longer than twelve weeks? Well, that's all right too.

Felicia gives the greatest advice on adjusting:

"When I first got back, I had a decision to make about getting married to the boy I'd been with for almost five years. Once I felt through prayer that was the right thing for me, I had to move on to the next part of my life. I had to figure out school, where we would live, jobs, and so on. I had no time to feel a lack of confidence. I relied a lot on my mother and eventually my husband to help me attack my tasks. I just took it one day and step at a time, and little by little, my life was getting organized, and I was on the track I wanted and knew I should be on. I didn't allow myself to worry about things that made me feel uncomfortable. For example—this is kind of a stupid example, but it represents what I'm talking about—when I first got home, the idea of the iPhone and all the new gadgets that were out there just made me feel over-whelmed. . . . Instead of worrying about figuring that all out, I just got a phone I was familiar with. When anything in my life made me feel that way, I just held off on trying to integrate it into my life until I could handle dealing with it." —Sister Felicia C.

Are you feeling a little bit of culture shock? Maybe a lot? Like I said, this indicates that you, sis, were an amazing missionary and gave your all while serving. Let me end with the beautiful words of Marielle:

"Allow yourself time to adjust. Remember when you stepped your first foot out in the mission field? Remember the first time you invited someone to read the Book of Mormon? Remember the first door you knocked on? Remember your first companion? Remember the first principle you attempted to teach? Were you perfect at it from the beginning? Do you remember the purpose of this life? To learn, to grow, to struggle, to come unto Christ. His grace is sufficient for all. Rely on Him. Trust Him. Follow Him. Be patient. Enjoy the journey and the learning experiences the Lord has and is blessing you with."—Sister Marielle N.

Chapter Two

OVERCOMING EMOTIONAL CULTURE SHOCK

"When you return from a mission, people want you to be the same person you were when you left. Friends and family expect that nothing has changed and sometimes even feel like it's their duty to help you return to 'normal.' The problem is, you have changed. You want to be different. You don't want to return to the person you were before . . . or, at the very least, you want to find a way to marry those two identities by finding a happy medium."
—Sister Amy J.

IN THIS CHAPTER WE WILL DISCUSS HOW TO EMOTIONally come home from your mission. This involves uniting the person you became with your home life. You do not have to and should not "throw the baby out with the bathwater" and abandon all of the good habits you created as a missionary. The purpose of this book is to help you take the principles learned on your mission home with you to continue to bless your life and bring you closer to the Lord. Lindsey describes this so beautifully:

"The process of becoming a missionary intentionally strips you of everything worldly you have ever used to define yourself. What music you listen to, the clothes you like to wear, favorite movies, hobbies, even foods. God, in a great deal of wisdom, reduces a missionary down to her most basic elements and eliminates all that is not absolutely essential. He removes the world, harmless or evil, distracting or damning. Then He, in the most intimate way, collects the pure elements that are left and, with His own two hands, sculpts you into a new person, just as much as you will let Him. That process is both painful and mind-blowingly awesome.

"Then He sends you back into the world, and you

look mostly like the old you. You have all the memories of the old you, and you find that you still like many of the things you used to like, but a good deal of life—now unstructured, not planned down to fifteen-minute intervals with a weekly rubric for documenting progress—feels incredibly awkward. How much of the new you will you keep? How much of the old you do you want back?"
—Sister Lindsay H.

The emotional transition home from a mission will be different for everyone. It will be impossible to say that after three months or a year things will feel "normal" again. I found that there were some adjustments the first few months of being home, and I expected that after I worked through those I would not encounter any other challenges. After a year of being home, I felt like I still was working to unite my missionary self with my "home" self. And can I be really honest with you? It wasn't until I had been home three years that I really felt like me. In some ways I still feel like I am adjusting from my service! Don't worry—during those first few years, I wasn't just sitting around whining and feeling bad for myself (although my mom, sister, and husband might disagree). I got married, graduated from college, remodeled a house, started my career, and got pregnant. And somehow during all of those years and experiences, during lots of prayer and temple attendance, I felt like I was able to be Andrea—the returned sister missionary. Not Andrea, the pre-missionary girl; or Sister Faulkner, the sister missionary; but Andrea, a returned sister missionary who knew who she was and felt confident about it.

Tell Me about It, SISTER

66 I got extremely ill on my mission. I had wanted to go on a mission my whole life, but four months into my mission I got really sick. The doctors couldn't figure out what was wrong with me. I was depressed that my body wouldn't let me serve. I stuck it out as long as I could, but my mission president sent me home at eleven months to get better. When I got home, I was bitter that my mission wasn't like everyone told me it would be. For years after my mission, I had a hard time feeling the Spirit and having faith in

God, especially because I was so ill and we couldn't figure out what was wrong with me. I saw over thirty doctors for seven years until I finally got my diagnosis: Lyme disease. It has now been five years since my diagnosis (twelve years total illness), and I have been all over the country finding correct doctors and treatments.

"I feel angry sometimes, but grateful too for the lessons I have learned from being sick. I was pretty naive before my mission. I thought I had all of the answers. But when it came down to it, I had never had to ask myself the really tough questions for my own life. I was soon brought to a world of humility, repentance, and the Atonement.

"On my mission I kept getting blessings when I was really sick. Every time I got a blessing, the elder would say, 'You must get to know the Savior.' It made me angry because that had nothing to do with getting well! I wanted guidance on doctors, medicine, or healing. But it came over and over: 'You must get to know the Savior.' It has taken me a long time to understand why my blessings said that, and I'm sure I'll continue to learn. But I think of the story of Moses and the sick people that could look at the serpent staff to get well, yet they wouldn't look because of the easiness of the way. I have relied so heavily on doctors, medicine, the Internet, and many other types of healing, but I forget that the Savior is the ultimate healer. He knows, more than any doctor on this earth, what I need to get better. And I know He doesn't like to see me suffer. He wants me to be happy even more than I want me to be happy. I know this now.

"I still look at my mission as a time of suffering and sadness. But I also look at it as the turning point in my life when I became softened to really understand the gospel of Jesus Christ. Without my mission, I would still be giving cookie-cutter answers to questions in Relief Society. But now I can just feel giddy because of all that I have learned and will continue to learn. How lucky am I?" —Anonymous

Letting Go of the Five-Year Plan

When I graduated from high school, I wrote down a five-year plan. I mapped out college, my major, a study abroad program, and a mission. And I followed it! Then, at the end of my mission, I created a new five-year plan to carry me through the next few years of my life. My plan had worked so well to this point, I figured I might as well map out my next five years! After my mission, I pushed and pushed to make the things happen on my new five-year plan. I would pray and think, "Why am I not happy?" and then I would continue to push to go in a certain direction, not because it felt right, but because it was how I had expected things to happen. Often I pushed for things to happen even when they felt frustrating and challenging. I did this with goals like receiving a master's degree, where I should live, and at what point I should get married. At times I wondered why Heavenly Father wasn't communicating with me. Why wasn't He directing my life like He had when I served a mission?

Looking back I see how stubborn I was and how obvious it was that God was directing my life; I just refused to sit back, be quiet, and enjoy the blessings He was trying to offer me. Doctrine and Covenants 4:3 says, "Therefore, if ye have desires to serve God ye are called to the work." My bishop in college shared this scripture with me when I asked him if he thought I should fill out mission papers. He explained to me that one of the ways the Lord communicates the right path for our lives is by giving us the desire to pursue a particular course. I had been given desires to do many things when returning home from a mission that were not on the five-year map I had created. I had a difficult time trusting those desires because they were in contrast to what I had *expected* to be doing.

It has been exactly five years since I returned home from my mission, and I marvel at the way my life has unfolded. I am so happy with everything I have been blessed with. At the same time, my experiences after a mission have taken me in a direction that in many ways has not lined up with the plan I had mapped out for myself. Setting goals is and will always be a way to draw closer to the Lord; do not stop setting goals! But we will always run into trouble when we try to push the Lord out of the way to meet a goal we assume we should be accomplishing. Our lives as missionaries were unique; we were striving for an ideal of perfection. Sometimes, readjusting to a less-than-ideal life can be jolting, but we must learn to make the adjustment. As Joseph Campbell said, "We must be willing to let go of the life we planned, so as to have the life that is waiting for us."

The biggest part of emotionally returning home from a mission will be letting go of expectations of how we thought things would be when we arrived home. There is a great life waiting for you, and the key is to learn to let go and embrace it. So, as we begin our little journey together, I invite you to put down the five-year plan and allow God to touch your heart. I promise you that the plan God will reveal to you will be greater than any you have created.

Mission Buddies

I always get so excited in the book of Alma in the Book of Mormon when Alma runs into the sons of Mosiah one day while doing missionary work. They were his mission buddies! They had been there with him during his conversion, and they were still "his brethren in the Lord" (Alma 17:1–2). They had shared the most powerful experience possible together, a conversion to the Lord. There is great strength in keeping in touch with the people you knew while you were a set-apart representative of the Lord. I often think about the two mission presidents I served under, whom I love and respect, and sometimes wonder, "Would they be proud of the choices I have made since I left their watch?" That accountability to those we served with can be humbling and productive.

It will be natural when returning from your mission to talk about and find joy in the things associated with your time in the field. There is no greater feeling than being at a mission reunion, reuniting with the people who were present for some of the most meaningful moments of your life. If you served in another country or with a different culture, you will probably crave the food, language, and attitudes you grew to love. (In fact, I am wearing a pair of Nauvoo sweatpants I purchased as a missionary right now while I am typing!) All of this means you were a great missionary, one who loved the work and the people you served with as well as the people you taught. Good for you! Just another reason why you are a total babe!

There can, however, be a concern when missionaries come home and immerse themselves in the people and culture of where they served to avoid new and slightly unfamiliar opportunities. Marcy found strength in associating with her former companions but also found there were limits to those benefits:

"I got together with my RM friends and 'talked mission' a lot. We still get together and reminisce about those days. I think it's important to remember that life post-mission is different, and although you may not feel that same spiritual high, your mission doesn't have to mark the 'best eighteen months of your life.' There's a lot to look forward to in the future: marriage and family, for example!" —Sister Marcy L.

As Marcy found, occasionally reminiscing about the mission is great, but excessively clinging onto mission memories may hold returned missionaries back from having new and different experiences that at first might force them out of their comfort zones.

A New Definition of Self

Think of how the leaders of the Church have established guidelines for missionaries to help their investigators convert to the gospel of Jesus Christ and not to just the missionaries. How do they do that? They ask that missionaries bring ward members to lessons, not stay longer than 30–40 minutes at any one lesson, and get the recent converts involved in their ward organizations soon after being baptized. As missionaries, we place a high priority on helping investigators truly convert to Christ and His message and not just to the missionaries and their friendship.

Don't you think our journey home from a mission should be the same? We should leave our mission field with a more devout testimony of Jesus Christ's Church rather than a testimony of the place, people, or members we served with. Just as missionaries are a conduit to bring Christ to the lives of God's children, missions and the experiences we have while serving are a way for us to better receive the gospel of Jesus Christ in our own lives.

The same principle can be seen at the occasional youth testimony meeting. Often times, people refer to these jokingly as "friendimony meetings." Youth will get up and begin to bear their testimonies but only focus on the people they love. What they are doing is associating the feelings of the Spirit with the friends and leaders who have touched them, not realizing that what they have really felt is the power of eternal truths.

Bailey puts it perfectly:

"By not defining myself solely as a returned missionary and choosing to pursue other interests, [I gained] a
sense of purpose." —Sister Bailey C.

There are two main reasons it is detrimental to place too much focus
on our missions and not on the eternal truths we learned while serving.

1. A mentality of focusing on the physical culture of your mission
and not on the spiritual lessons learned will leave you empty. It will take
your energy away from spiritual progression, and that is precisely why you
were so happy as a missionary: you had the Spirit! The gospel requires
constant progression.

"For behold, thus saith the Lord God: I will give unto
the children of men line upon line, precept upon precept, here a little and there a little; and blessed are those
who hearken unto my precepts, and lend an ear unto my
counsel, for they shall learn wisdom; for unto him that
receiveth I will give more; and from them that shall say,
We have enough, from them shall be taken away even
that which they have" (2 Nephi 28:30).

2. Your goal as a returned missionary is not to get to know the culture of your mission better. I am not suggesting that going to mission
reunions, spending time with mission companions, or continuing to love
the culture you served in is a bad thing. No! Not at all. My mission companions are some of my greatest friends in the world. We get together
regularly, have parties, go to dinner, and even take trips together. When
life is challenging we pray and fast for one another. What I am suggesting is that if you are so busy with mission companions, staying in touch
with members from your area, and finding people to speak your mission
language with, you are going to miss out on opportunities socially and
spiritually that you have to look *forward to.* Your local singles ward needs
you! They need your service and friendship. And sister, those boys need
you to show up to activities so they can ask you on dates and tell you how
pretty you are! There are college programs waiting for your applications;
bosses that want to hire capable, stellar women like you; and friends who
need to feel the Spirit you are filled with as a fresh returned missionary.

A Pattern of Growth

"I would give the same advice to sisters who are returning from their missions and to those who are leaving for their missions: forget yourself and be open to change. The times I struggled most as a returned missionary were the times that I couldn't stop thinking about myself and my own worries and concerns. Choosing to accept that you changed on your mission but are not solely defined by the fact that you served one helps too."
—Sister Bailey C.

Your goal is not just to come home from a mission but to make a transition home that brings your mission home with you. Bringing your mission home with you means accepting that your time as a full-time servant of the Lord is over but holding onto the strength in Christ you found while you served. The balance between mission and home life will come as we are "anxiously engaged in a good cause, and do many things of [our] own free will, and bring to pass much righteousness" (Doctrine and Covenants 58:27). In other words, don't stop doing the things that brought you joy on your mission: exercising, reading your scriptures, praying with a purpose, serving others, working hard, and so on. At the same time, make sure you find other worthwhile activities to invest your time in. Set goals for school and work, and spend time with your local singles ward and reacquainting with friends and family.

As time goes on, you will naturally find that you are growing in a way you had not imagined you would. Any feelings of discomfort will open your heart with greater compassion for others. Over time you will start to recognize that your mission was just one of a long list of experiences you will treasure. You will begin to take who you were from before your mission and the lessons learned on your mission and become a new, improved version of yourself.

The truth is, sister, you being a returned sister missionary is just the *beginning* of what you are going to do. Use your mission as an MTC for the life ahead of you. Coming home and uniting your mission and home lives requires the Savior and His love. This process is another opportunity to get to know Him.

Reading Suggestions

+   Henry B. Eyring. "Where Is the Pavilion?" *Ensign*, Nov. 2012.

- Quentin L. Cook. "What E'er Thou Art, Act Well Thy Part: Avoid Wearing Masks That Hide Identity." CES Fireside, 4 Mar. 2012.

Self-Analysis Quiz

Response Key

 1 = never   4 = almost always
 2 = sometimes   5 = always
 3 = often

Please use the key to honestly answer these statements:

_____ I use my time wisely.

_____ I use the skills I learned on my mission (hard work, perseverance, faith) in my scholastic and vocational pursuits.

_____ I go to the Lord with questions about what type of education or career I should pursue.

_____ I feel comfortable associating with people outside of my mission circle (such as companions, members, and investigators).

_____ I am continuing to progress spiritually like I did on my mission.

_____ I rely on the Savior to help me as I adjust home from my mission.

Journal Prompts

How can I best use my time to progress as a returned sister missionary? How have I been able to unite the person I became on my mission with my life at home? What have I brought home with me from my time serving? What has my experience of coming home from a mission taught me?

_____

_____

_____

_____

_____

_____

_____

_____

_____

_____

_____

_____

_____

_____

_____

_____

_____

_____

_____

_____

_____

_____

_____

_____

_____

_____

_____

_____

Chapter Three

HOTTIE WITH AN RSM BODY

> "When coming home, you are not only older than many of the boys, but you feel a significant pressure that you are missing the marriage boat. Young men also have mixed responses when you tell them you are an RM. Many have a preconceived notion of what a returned sister missionary is supposed to look and act like. Unfortunately, this is not always favorable, and I did not enjoy being placed in this category. I found it difficult at times to connect with girls, as I felt like my frame of reference was so different. In other words, I felt like a misfit in multiple settings."
> —Sister Brittany C.

YES! THE CHAPTER YOU'VE BEEN WAITING FOR. The one where we talk about looking good as a returned sister missionary. I was originally going to title this chapter "Work It, Girl," and then I worried about offending you, so I switched it to "Dress and Appearance." But after much deliberation, I have settled on "Hottie with an RSM Body." I hope it communicates my enthusiasm for how good you're looking as an RSM.

The Skinny Jeans Meltdown

The day I came home from my mission, my sister was so excited to take me shopping and introduce me to the new exciting fashions I had missed. It was 2007, and flats and skinny jeans were all the rage. I asked to postpone the trip, but she explained that my frumpy P-day jeans and running shoes just weren't going to cut it for one more day. So with hesitation, I allowed her to take me to a trendy store with loud music and fashionable sales attendants. I apprehensively went into the dressing room with a few pairs of tapered skinny jeans she had picked out. Let's just say the size she had remembered me wearing before my mission had changed over a year and a half of dinner appointments and zone breakfasts. But I was determined to get myself in these things. It was me versus the skinny jeans, and it eventually came down to me having to lie down on the floor to stuff myself into them. (You know, like they do in the movies? This really happened.) When I stood up to look in the mirror I felt anything but skinny. Tears began to stream down my face; I wished for nothing more than to sneak out the back door and back into my pleated mid-calf skirt and clunky mission shoes.

At first, wearing my mission clothes and living like I was a missionary while I was home seemed easier and happier than having to wear something different. Your dress and appearance while you're a missionary are important because you are a representative of the Lord, but your priority is serving in your area and not taking extreme amounts of time for your personal look. For that reason, many missionaries get used to not devoting much time or effort to their personal appearance. But, sister, you are home! Good news: You no longer need to wear the same button-down, wrinkle-free tops *every single day*. You can take it up a notch and bring a little more fashion into your life. Not only are you *allowed* to do this, I completely recommend it! If you come home and set a pattern of ignoring your appearance, it will be difficult to make adjustments later in life. So, let's get down to business on how to get looking like a ten again. Yowza!

Establish Your Brand

When we see those pretty golden arches shining on a street corner, we know what we are going to get—yummy, quick, cheap food. We understand exactly what will be handed to us when we pull through that drive-thru. For better or for worse, McDonalds has branded those golden arches forever in our minds. We also have a brand. The way we dress and take care of our bodies is how we brand ourselves. Our physical appearance is an outward demonstration of our spirit. Our hair, choice of jewelry, makeup, and shoes are only material objects, but when put together they represent what is important to us and how we spend our time. They are the first things people judge our character by. What do people think when they see us? Are we getting dressed with the intention of feeling confident about ourselves? Are we getting dressed with the intention of attracting the opposite sex? Do we spend an appropriate amount of time considering how our physical appearance and spiritual life line up? Our physical appearance, or the way we brand ourselves, will influence how we feel about ourselves. How we feel about ourselves influences our receptiveness to the Spirit and the way we treat others.

I firmly believe that, with a little TLC and a lot of time talking with the Lord, we will not have to feel "old," "out of place," or "outdated" as a returned sister missionary. The Heavenly Father I love and know would not want one of His daughters to feel that way. He wants our lives to be filled with confidence and light; He wants our physical appearances to be another way for Him to communicate His love to us.

There Is a Time and a Place

"It's important to dress modestly after returning from a mission. But remember that we can improve a little. There are cuter shoes out there than those we used to walk miles and miles in the mission field. It's okay to wear more accessories and perfume. The hair doesn't need to be low maintenance and boring anymore. Dancing again is fun! This will not only help in the dating scenario but will also boost your confidence." —Sister Dri M.

A few months after returning home from my mission, I applied and was lucky enough to get a job teaching at the MTC. When I accepted the job, I immediately called my mother. She, an RSM herself, had taught Japanese at the MTC when she returned home, and I knew she would just be gushing about how proud she was of me, right? Well, kind of. She was very proud of me and quick to express that, but what immediately followed was this: "Andrea, I know that working at the MTC will require you to dress in missionary standards while at work, but let's get one thing straight. Don't you ever wear those clothes outside of your work environment. When you are done with your shift, walk immediately to your car, drive home, and change. You aren't a missionary anymore, so you shouldn't be spending the whole day walking around looking like one!"

At the time I definitely felt like she was overreacting, but looking back I think that is the greatest advice anyone gave me as a returned sister missionary. Just like it would be uncomfortable to see guys in your classes and at work wearing their mission suits, make sure you stay far, far away from those mission clothes when you return. There might be pieces you wear to church or with jeans, but take some time when you get home to find some cute new items to update your wardrobe. Have fun doing this! You didn't shop for a year and a half; you deserve it! In the reading suggestions at the end of the chapter, I have listed a few of my favorite "modest" fashion blogs. These are great resources for fashion direction when you are feeling a little lost. Check out the blogs, see what styles you feel comfortable with, and then begin to follow that blog for continued inspiration.

In July of 2013, the Church updated the standards on how a sister missionary should dress while in the field.[2] More patterns and colors and fewer restrictions were implemented. "Hallelujah!" was my response when I first heard news of this—I am sure you had a similar reaction. Although these new guidelines loosen up the look for sisters, you still need to be careful to not continue dressing just like a sister missionary would. Men in the Church have been taught not to be attracted to sister missionaries—we don't want to look like the one type of girl they aren't supposed to be interested in!

Shop Till You Drop

Shopping you say . . . shopping?! If this word sounds scary right now, then let me sympathize. When I returned home from my mission, one of the hardest things for me was not knowing how to shop. It sounds silly I know, but when you take off your nametag it feels like you are taking off your identity. For quite some time I battled to find a balance in expressing my personality through my appearance while trying to maintain dignity and modesty. In other words, I didn't know how to be me and still dress like a returned sister missionary "should" dress. It really upset me that I felt so different, and I would feel anxious whenever I went with friends or family to look for new clothes, things for my home, or things for others. For some reason, experiences I had on my mission changed my taste, and now I wasn't sure what I liked. The insecurity of not knowing what you like or what you want is not a great feeling—in any area of our lives. I suggest that just because it seems uncomfortable to update your personal appearance does not mean it isn't a good thing to do. Even though it was at times difficult to face having to buy new clothes, something I used to love to do, I think it was good for me to not stop trying to look like my best self just because it made me a little uncomfortable in the process.

Don't shy away from updating your look. Dedicating a moderate amount of time to your dress and appearance will help you feel confident and beautiful, just how you should feel. Get your hair done; buy some new lip gloss or nail polish. Recognize what makes you feel happy and confident, and go after it. Face those skinny jeans head on, sister; you can do it!

In order to ease my shopping woes, I created a list of questions I ask myself while shopping to help with any anxiety and to create room for me to express myself in my appearance. And, sister, I want to share them with you. I hope you will find them helpful as well. Give them a try! Before purchasing any article of clothing, I ask myself these four questions. If the answer is a no or a maybe to any of these, don't buy it! It's not worth it!

- Does this article of clothing represent who I am as a daughter of God?

- Do I feel pretty when I wear this?

- Do I feel like this clothing accentuates my feminine qualities?

- Would I want to put this on and wear it out of the store?

Pretty good, right? I know! Try it next time; let me know how it goes.

Christin Buck SUPERSTAR

Christin Buck and I served together in the Illinois Nauvoo Mission, which makes us bosom buddies. She is a total beauty who radiates light and goodness. Since returning home, Christin has earned a bachelor's and master's degree in marriage and family therapy. She now works as a licensed therapist, specifically with young adults. To help put herself through school, Christin worked at a retail store that primarily supplies clothing for sister missionaries. She is to thank for dressing a lot of the world's sisters! Her style is always bright, and she always knows just how to help a sister in need. Let her give you a few tips.

Q *Did you find it challenging to be confident in your appearance as a returned sister missionary?*

A I always had respect for girls who had a current modest look, but I felt that they were few and far between. It seemed to me that you could either be cute or you could look like your mom, and I did not know how to balance that. For me, that has always been a struggle, and it's something I'm constantly refining and looking to improve. There is a big difference between being covered and expressing who you are through fashion. It's also really important to be confident when you are dating, and if I feel like I look good, confidence seems natural.

Q *How have you been able to find a balance between trying to look your best and not placing all of your time and energy into your appearance?*

A It is important to discover your own personal style. What kinds of things do you want to be presenting to others? Establishing that really saves a lot of time. You can see something online or in a store and know if it fits into your personal style almost instantly. Any time used for self-discovery in this area is really a good investment of your time. I read a book once that made me list five words that I would like to describe me. I decided that one of my words was *happy*, and from then on I started using a lot more color in my wardrobe because it made me feel bright and happy. It's not enough to just be modest.

Q *I love the five words! So, what are common mistakes you see returned sister missionaries make when it comes to dressing and taking care of themselves?*

A What I did was being too "safe." Hopefully the new dress and grooming guidelines for sister missionaries have done away with that, but in the past I felt that I had to look like a sister missionary to be nearer to God. There are a lot of girls who never "come home" from the mission. I think that it's important to ditch the "sister look" as soon as possible. Get highlights, wear skinny jeans, paint your nails—do something—but please ditch the boring collared shirts and plaid skirts as soon as humanly possible.

Q *How has placing energy into your "look" given you confidence in other areas of your life?*

A Putting energy into my look has really paid off in dating. Any time I tweaked something or switched things up a bit, I would always attract new men. The more I have come into myself through my wardrobe and even by reaching an ideal body weight, the more I was able to attract guys that were more ideal for me. If you aren't being asked out, the first thing that I would take a look at is what you are presenting.

Q *Is there anything else you would like to share with returned sister missionaries about dress and appearance?*

A Dress and appearance is something that you can always be improving on in an appropriate way. I don't think I've ever been extreme, but I am always looking for ways to do better, and I think that it's important to listen carefully to feedback from others.

Work It, Girl!

"If you have trouble feeling the Spirit, remember to do the things that bring the Spirit—scriptures, prayer, and especially attending the temple. Also, remember that your body is the conductor that the Spirit uses to speak to your spirit. If you don't get enough sleep, healthy food, and exercise, your body will have a harder time conducting the promptings of the Spirit. We have to do the things He has asked us to do or we won't be able to feel His love for us as strongly as He wants us to feel it."
—Sister Rose K.

On your mission you were required to work out thirty minutes every morning. For a lot of sisters, this might be the first time in their lives they had a regular workout schedule. For others, this might have been a significant decrease compared to their level of activity before their missions. No matter what you did before your mission, use the new routine of daily exercise after your mission. Set exercise goals, join a local gym or sports team, and make it a priority to exert yourself physically almost every single day. Whether or not you like to be physically active, doing so will allow you to release endorphins, it will give you a routine you can rely on, and it will give you a way to stay busy with good activities. Exercising will help you feel pretty and make you more confident in dating, and with your world being turned upside down, it will give you the emotional stability you just might feel you are lacking.

> "Take care of yourself. Especially if you gained weight on your mission, take the time to find a healthy balance in life post-mission. Remember that the true success of missionaries isn't how many converts they had but if they are still living what they taught five, ten, or twenty years after the mission. It is all about applying what you learned to real life." —Anonymous

I love what this sister has to say about taking care of ourselves. It is easy to gain weight as a missionary. Weight gain can be a long-term concern not only for our self-esteem but also for health reasons. Heavenly Father wants you to be able to feel His love and strength always. Don't allow fifteen pounds of mission baggage to stand in the way of being able to feel God's love.

Jamie Pyatt SUPERSTAR

Jamie Stubblefield Pyatt is a pillar of strength. She has served twice as a Young Women president and is the type of woman who is constantly opening up her home, her wallet, and her heart to women in need. She holds both a bachelor's and master's degree in social work from Brigham Young University and has worked professionally as a therapist for LDS Family Therapy and her own private counseling practice.

Jamie served her mission in McAllen, Texas, and Honduras. She and her husband, Dave, live with their daughter, Mackenzie, in San Diego, California. She has an incredible tan and spends all of her free time doing things like paddleboarding and playing beach volleyball. She's a total babe!

Q *Jamie, what advice do you have for returned sister missionaries about their dress and appearance?*

A My advice is just to do your best with what you've got! I am 5'11" and grew up never feeling like a feminine person because I was so much bigger than everyone around me. I served most of my mission in the McAllen, Texas, area, Spanish speaking. This means I had homemade tortillas every day, sugar soda, and anything else that the people thought would help me gain thirty pounds while serving. My missionary attire lent me to barely even noticing my weight gain! I had been an extremely competitive swimmer and involved in lots of triathlons before my mission, so I did know I was out of shape. However, I was in the best spiritual shape of my life at that point, so I just didn't worry about it a whole lot.

During my final interview with my mission president, he asked me if I had any concerns about going home and dating and going to school. At this moment, all spirituality went out the window and I started to cry. I hadn't thought much about school and dating in those eighteen months, and now he brought it all to the surface. I said, "I have gained thirty pounds; I probably won't do much dating and will get the best grades of my life." Both proved true. I didn't date a whole lot that first semester back, and I got the best grades of my undergraduate career that semester. However, I don't think I didn't date because I had gained thirty pounds. I came home and created a sense of balance in my life. I started working out daily, I didn't buy lard for homemade tortillas, I found a new addiction to Diet Coke, and I lost the weight. I decided that looking and feeling good wasn't about getting a date, but it was about being my best. So, sisters, do your best!

Q *I love this honest story! You have such great style and always look so good. How did you find confidence in your style and feel comfortable with your physical appearance after serving?*

A The answer to this question is much deeper than Seven jeans or Steve Madden boots. It goes back to something we all started reciting when we were twelve years old: "We are daughters of a Heavenly Father, who loves us, and we love Him."[3] I find confidence in my style and physical appearance because I know who I am. Whether you show up to my house and I am still in my pajamas at four in the afternoon or I am having a day where I feel I can rock a pencil skirt and heels, you still get the same Jamie: one who believes she is a daughter of a Heavenly Father who loves her, and she loves Him.

Q *Beautiful. Thank you so much! How do you feel like the way we treat our physical bodies affects our spiritual progression?*

A We have been taught that the body is a temple. It is what houses our spirits, and it is where the Holy Ghost dwells, which actually means we are sacred beings. I can't picture ever going to the temple and saying, "Ew . . . look at that stained-glass window!" Or, "It's so ugly!" Or, "Why do they cast Moroni in a gold color? Gold is so nineties!" Sounds ridiculous, right? But when it comes to our own temples, we never hesitate to focus on our flaws. I have tried to imagine how my Heavenly Father might feel when He hears me talking about my legs—that run, walk, and help me magnify my calling as a woman—as fat or ugly. I wonder what He thinks when I complain about my stringy hair. Again, it sounds ridiculous, but we have all engaged in this negative thinking, and when we believe this about our body, how can the Spirit truly dwell with us? We are beautiful—every single one of us. I may never make the cover of a magazine, but I am beautiful because I am created in God's image, and that *can't* be ugly!

Your Body—A Conduit for the Spirit

"Don't be afraid to take care of yourself. Going from serving 24-7 to reflecting on yourself and your own identity can be overwhelming, but you can't fill empty vessels. If you want to keep serving and having an impact, you've got to fill your own vessel first and make sure you're taken care of." —Sister Juliet L.

I would also like to point out the importance of being "moderate" in all things. Don't ever use starvation, unhealthy amounts of exercise, vomiting, or unhealthy supplements to encourage weight loss. These habits are harmful to you and to your spirit. If you gained a little weight on your mission, do not ever use unhealthy tactics to get rid of it. If you are now considering or using any of these eating habits, see a doctor or counsel with a leader immediately.

Striving to be beautiful inside and out has more to do with loving and caring for ourselves than with attracting a member of the opposite sex. The Heavenly Father I know would not want His daughters to feel unattractive, insecure, or left behind in any area of their lives. God loves us as His daughters and intends for us to feel valued and appreciated. If your physical appearance is stopping you from feeling His love, I hope you will consider making changes in your lifestyle. On the other hand, if you feel like you are spending too much of your focus on physical appearance and neglecting your spirit, I hope this chapter will help you achieve a healthy balance. In my life, I have found that I am happiest when I am confident in my physical appearance for the right reasons.

A bishop on my mission once said, "When we fast, we are showing our physical body that our spiritual body is in charge." Ever since I have always thought, "I want my spirit to be in charge!" I relate this hierarchy to all things physical in my life. When we take care of our bodies in a proper way, we are showing our physical body that our spiritual body is in charge and wants to shine through. We are showing our physical body that healthy eating, proper exercise, and attractive dress are a way to feel God's love. Sister, you are beautiful! Honest. You are a real knockout.

Reading Suggestions

+ Doctrine & Covenants 88
+ www.caraloren.com

- • www.barefootblonde.com
- • www.pinkpeonies.com

Self-Analysis Quiz

Response Key

    1 = never   4 = almost always

    2 = sometimes   5 = always

    3 = often

Please use the key to honestly answer these statements:

_____ I feel confident in my dress and appearance.

_____ My physical appearance reflects my spiritual strength.

_____ I take care of myself physically so that others are attracted to me.

_____ I have healthy eating and exercise habits.

_____ I allow feelings of doubt and insecurity to affect my life.

Journal Prompts

How am I uniquely beautiful? What has the Lord blessed me with physically? What is one thing I can do physically to freshen up my look?

_____

_____

_____

_____

_____

_____

_____

_____

_____

_____

_____

_____

_____

_____

_____

_____

_____

_____

_____

_____

_____

_____

_____

_____

_____

_____

_____

_____

_____

_____

Chapter Four

BACK IN THE DATING GAME

"It is essential to understand the nature of our Heavenly Father and that His desire is for us to be happy—happy despite challenging circumstances that are beyond our realm of control. I thought I would be married before turning thirty, and it is still my desire. However, I don't doubt the Lord's timetable. I keep the commandments and know I am entitled to all the blessings the Lord has in store for me. I love my career, and I love the callings I have held in the Church. I value the lessons I have learned as a single daughter of our Heavenly Father." —Sister Natalie B.

Me? Awkward? Never . . .

THE DAY AFTER RETURNING FROM MY MISSION, A friend from my home ward came over. We had dated very briefly the year before my mission, and he was a great friend to me while I was serving. He invited me to dinner at his house that next night with his family. I went, feeling a little nervous but comfortable being around old friends. While at dinner, his family was so sweet to ask me questions about my mission and Nauvoo, where I served, and his dad started to tell me about their family history and ancestors who had lived there. When the dinner was over, I had neglected to pay any attention to this boy and found myself in the back room looking at genealogical charts with his dad! What?! Oops . . . so awkward. Needless to say, I wasn't asked over for dinner or for any other kind of date ever again! That day I really wondered how I was going to transition from gung-ho sister missionary to someone who was comfortable dating and moving toward marriage. I wasn't exactly off to a great start!

In the last chapter we talked about how the way we treat our bodies

41

physically will contribute to our spiritual progression. Well, now that we are looking like babes and feeling stylish (as well as feeling all spiritual!), it's time to talk about dating. Here's the thing: Being a sister missionary is amazing, but being married in the temple and committing your life to someone is the greatest joy we can have on this earth. Prepare to be married in the temple. Think about the activities you are engaged in daily and assess whether or not they are leading you to have opportunities to date. (Use the quiz at the end of chapter 5 to do this.) Just as you will never commit anyone on your mission to baptism if you don't open your mouth and share your message, find people to teach, and invite them to make changes in their lives, *you will never get married if you don't date.* There, I said it! It is the truth. I am sorry I had to say it, but I am not going to dance around the issue. I think sometimes we try to ignore that reality, but if we are not putting ourselves in a position to date exclusively, we will never be placing ourselves in a position to develop potential marriage relationships.

In a 2008 CES Devotional, Elder Earl C. Tingey taught, "It is a truth from heaven that you are not to be alone."[4] We know that Satan is attacking the home. He would want us to believe that we will never find love or eternal happiness. We know that the world has a skewed perception of dating and marriage. God's plan is true and right. We are not expected to be alone forever. We are often promised that even if we are alone during this life, if we remain faithful we will be blessed with eternal companionship. This is a beautiful promise, and we need to develop the skills and knowledge in this life to make ourselves into someone worthy to be ready to be with a wonderful companion. So regardless of *when* we get married, we need to prepare for when that time comes. So, sisters, let's get our marriage prep on.

Leave the Past Behind

"[After my mission] I really struggled to figure out what my next step was. I had decided on a major before going on a mission, but when I came home it just didn't feel right anymore. Socially I was struggling too. All my friends seemed confident, and dating seemed to come easily for them. I had struggled with confidence before my mission, and, while serving a mission strengthened that area immensely, I still felt inadequate, especially around the opposite sex. I struggled with my weight

and was also struggling emotionally. My mission helped to strengthen those things, but once thrown back into normal everyday life, I lost hold of the truths that I felt so deeply on my mission. If I had continued the good habits created on my mission, it would have helped a ton!"
—Sister Kim P.

I love how Kim says that on her mission she was able overcome certain things she had struggled with before serving. The challenge is to continue with that change after returning home. I remember watching closely when my older brother came home from a mission and chose different roommates, dating partners, and social activities. His heart had changed on a mission, and he wanted those changes to be reflected in his life. I remember feeling so impressed by how he quietly implemented the changes he had made on a mission in his new life at home.

Coming home from a mission is a great time to make long-term changes in our lives, especially when it comes to dating. If before your mission you weren't the girl in the ward who got to know any of the guys and you want that to change, now is the time. On the other hand, if you always dated guys who weren't worthy of your love, don't get near them. Pray to be strong as a returned sister missionary, and use the Atonement to be a better you—a you who deserves to date a respectful, kind, good, attractive priesthood holder. Because that *is* what you deserve!

Most people have bad relationship habits they have to work on and improve. Never feel like you are the only one who has trouble finding a date, keeping a boyfriend, or expressing your feelings. Your transition home from your mission is an ideal time to shed those bad dating habits and adopt new ones. Instead of coming home and blaming your imperfections on your mission, use your mission as a starting point to move forward.

You Are NOT ALONE

Out of two hundred returned sister missionaries surveyed, most reported they felt awkward in dating situations in the first year home from their mission. Over half reported that they felt uncomfortable "always, most of the time, or often." So it's not just you!

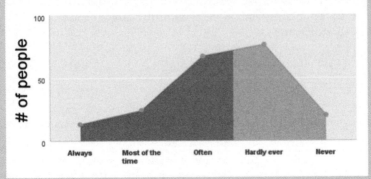

In the first year (1–12 months post-mission) of returning home from your mission, did you feel uncomfortable in dating situations?

The good news? When asked about their second year home from their mission, over 84 percent of the sisters surveyed said they "never or hardly ever" felt uncomfortable about their dating life. We can take two things away from this. First, it takes time to come home and turn the dating switch on again. On my mission, I remember doing everything I could to make sure I was never misinterpreted as flirting or trying to catch a guy's eye. It is natural that it will take a little time to get your groove back; you just have to work it—I mean work on it! Second, you aren't the only one who has ever felt a little uncomfortable on a date. Only 20 percent of sister missionaries surveyed "never" felt uncomfortable with dating after coming home.

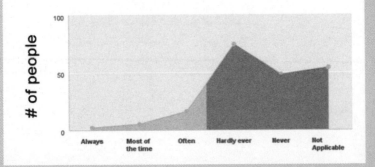

In the second year (12–24 months post-mission) of returning home from your mission, did you feel uncomfortable in dating situations?

We even asked these two hundred sisters about physical affection in dating relationships. Over 50 percent answered that yes, they did feel uncomfortable with physical affection in dating relationships. These statistics decreased dramatically when survey participants were asked about their second year home from their missions. These findings confirm that with time, dating and affection will become easier. They also confirm that you are not the only RSM who has felt too nervous to hold a boy's hand. We all have!

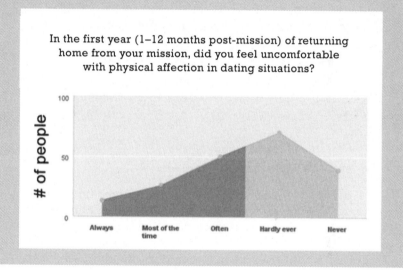

In the first year (1–12 months post-mission) of returning home from your mission, did you feel uncomfortable with physical affection in dating situations?

Tell Me about It, SISTER

"I was an awkward dater to begin with. I didn't kiss anyone until right before my mission. I have always been 'one of the guys' and had very close guy friends, just not boyfriends. I was not comfortable with physical affection, and it posed a pretty big challenge for me in dating. But again, this was a personal thing and not an effect of my mission. BYU was a little hard for me after my mission. On the majority of my group/double/blind dates, I was the oldest person, even older than all the guys. At twenty-four!

"I was very anxious to get on with my life and left for Washington, D.C., the day after graduation. I was almost twenty-nine when I got married, and I will say that the longer you are single, the more you start to second-guess your life. You question: Why, if you have done everything right, is this righteous desire not being fulfilled? I have not found the answer, and I continue to study the Atonement and hope and think along those lines even more now, dealing with recurrent pregnancy loss for the past two and a half years. The biggest lesson I have learned is that there isn't an end-all answer to our happiness. If we are operating on 'I'll be happy when I get a boyfriend' or 'when I get married' or 'when I have kids,' we won't magically be fixed when that desire is realized. However, I know my mission experience has given me the foundation and understanding to get through these trials." —Sister Robin M.

The Challenge of Being Single

"I didn't get married until I'd been home for eleven years, and I didn't date very much in all that time either. I got a lot of attention from nonmember guys and had many opportunities to wonder if a worthy priesthood holder would ever be interested in me. But I was also able to finish graduate school, work abroad, see the world, learn and grow, and have a lot of experiences that will surely benefit me for the rest of my life. The bottom line is that every stage of your life is just your life and will have its challenges and trials. 'If only I were _____, then I'd be happy' is never going to be true." —Sister Alyce L.

One of the hardest parts about being a single is feeling like you are never really happy. Do not fall into a pattern of thinking that marriage will solve all of your problems. It is neither productive nor true. Keep striving to be the kind of person who is worthy of someone great and wonderful who will take you to the temple.

I do not, however, want to underestimate the difficulty of being a single sister or brother in the Church. We are a family-oriented church, which can make a single member wonder, "What place do I have here?" You are not alone! Other sisters find it difficult to feel comfortable and happy as a single sister in the Church.

"I love the gospel. I loved my mission. I love my life. I wouldn't change any of it. However, on my mission we prayed about a million times a day and had the strong guidance from the Spirit. After coming home, that changed a little bit. I had to start going to school and working and being social. I have stayed active and close to the gospel and the Lord over the years, but as I've gotten a little older, it has been a little bit difficult to find my place in the Church and sometimes to remember to read my scriptures every night. My very best friends are learning about the gospel through the eyes of their children and teaching the gospel in a different way. We are a very family-oriented church, which is wonderful, but as an older single adult it's hard to know where you fit in." —Sister Jenna H.

"I have been home for over five years, and it has been very difficult to feel the guidance of the Spirit in my day-to-day life. I feel that as I get older, being a single member of the Church has become a challenge for me. Often I question my place in the Church." —Sister Jendar M.

"There are many times in life when people struggle to find what their 'real' purpose is. The roller coaster of life gets tricky and sometimes difficult when you are a single woman living and participating in a very family-oriented religion and you don't have a family of your own." —Sister Jill P.

When asked what she needed to hear as a returned sister missionary, Sara said:

"Even if you're twenty-seven and single, you are still part of the Lord's plan. You are not irrelevant in the gospel. A woman who is not married is still needed." — Sister Sara V.

I am grateful for the responses of friends and survey participants who honestly expressed the challenges of being single as an active Latter-day Saint. Just like Sara said, we need every sister in the Church. You fill a role that can only be filled by you, and your spirit blesses the lives of others every day. I promise. Being single and dating might bring you some of the most challenging experiences of your life. I hope in them you will find comfort in the Lord. I love you, sister! Keep reading for some of my very best dating advice!

Chapter Five

ANDREA'S GUIDE TO LOVE

"To you single women and men who wish to be married I say this, Do not give up hope. And do not give up trying. But do give up being obsessed with it. The chances are that if you forget about it and become anxiously engaged in other activities, the prospects will brighten immeasurably."[5] —Gordon B. Hinckley

AFTER A YEAR OF MARRIAGE, I HAD AN EPIPHANY. I realized that the same character flaws that made my relationships with my family, companions, and roommates challenging were also difficult in my marriage. What?! I will fully admit that I was under the impression that marrying the right person meant that my shortcomings would no longer be evident. I imagined that after I kissed my hunk over the alter, all of my tendencies to nag and get offended would magically disappear. (I know, I'm crazy.) This new view on life helped me understand that we set patterns with our relationships—all of them. If you have a pattern of being confrontational with those you date, this will not change when you are married. If you serve your roommates and family, you will also serve your spouse. See how it works? With that being said, I think dating is such a beautiful time to set healthy patterns of communication and learn how to really work on the character flaws that make our relationships hard.

In this chapter, I will give you my very best dating advice. I understand that, after that family history story, you might be a little leery of any dating tips from me, but, as always, I have enlisted the help of our returned sister missionary friends to bring you a little dating advice. So here it is: Andrea's Guide to Love.

49

Put Yourself Out There

"Going out on every date I was asked on helped me. I was able to date a lot and really paint a picture of what type of man I wanted to marry. After I graduated from college, I volunteered to work at the temple. That was amazing and also a huge help in not allowing any voids to open up in my spiritual life. Lucky for me, it was also where I met my husband." —Anonymous

We often shove all dating responsibility onto men and think, "If I am living righteously, one day someone will show up at my door ready to marry me." Right? We tend to do that, especially in the Church culture, where men are expected to be the initiators in relationships. I think it is also safe to say that as women we often like to romanticize this process. I am no exception. For example, I *thoroughly* enjoy watching chick flicks on Netflix and reading Jane Austen novels in my pajamas. Dreaming of the perfect love and marriage and all of the attention and sweetness you might someday receive . . . why wouldn't we love doing that? Activities like these can revitalize me and help me be happy. But I would argue that spending repeated days and nights with other girls, watching movies and dreaming up the perfect romance, are not "marriage prep" settings and should not become a recurring Friday night activity. You need to actually be out there, meeting real-life men!

Dreaming of romance and being out on dates are two different things. Remember in Young Women when your teachers asked you to make a list of all of the things you wanted in your future husband? I think my list had fifty-seven things on it—things like "plays the piano," "really hot," "really athletic," and "does not wear sneakers with jeans." It is safe to say, if I had held out waiting for a man to date who fulfilled my dream list, I would be spending *a lot* of Friday nights in my pj's watching Netflix. Don't wait to find the perfect guy before going out on dates; instead, keep your moral standards high but your expectations reasonable while putting yourself out there to date good guys until you find the one who is perfect for you.

Give Those Poor Guys a Break

My husband often talks about being a nervous fourteen-year-old boy, brand new at stake dances. He describes the swarms of girls standing huddled together with their backs to the world, making it impossible for anyone to come and talk to them, let alone ask them to dance. You can just visualize these girls moving around the dance floor like a herd of cattle! I remember being one of them. The worst part about this picture is that these fourteen-year-old girls were probably dying that no one ever asked them to dance and had no idea what their actions were communicating to those terrified boys. Without taking away anything from men, let's think about what responsibility we have. One of our most important responsibilities is simply to be open to dating! Make it easy for people to ask you out. Be honest with yourself about your actions toward members of the opposite sex. What message are you communicating? Ask a close friend or family member to help you understand what your actions communicate. Sister, are you huddled with the other girls, making it uncomfortable for men to come talk to you? I hope not!

A lot of times girls arrange themselves into social "security blankets" with other women, because of the fear of having to talk to someone new. I love what Carey says about how her mission made her feel confident in dating situations:

> "I served an honorable mission and worked very hard. This gave me confidence. I came home and was closer to the Lord than before. This gave me confidence. I attracted members of the opposite sex who saw spiritual strength in me. This gave me confidence. I tried my best to take care of myself and get good grades in school. This gave me confidence. I went on to grad school and was also able to use skills and language used in the mission. This gave me confidence. Every day I am alive, I feel so grateful for the opportunity I had to serve a full-time mission. I feared never being asked out when I came home from my mission because I would be older, more serious, and so on, but I found the opposite to be true. Surrounding myself with those who loved and appreciated sister missionaries helped and also gave me confidence." —Sister Carey L.

Putting yourself out there involves showing up! Make time to go to institute and Church activities, and find social activities where people you would want to date will be. These activities exist in the Church to give you an opportunity to shine. Sister, rock those singles dances, institute classes, and linger longers! If you don't show up, no one will ever meet you, see how great you are, fall in love, ask you to marry them, etcetera.

What If He Doesn't Ask You Out?

So, you say, "I am going to all of these activities and putting my best foot forward and *nothing* is happening!" This is sadly the case for a lot of us. There are some women who do not get asked out on a lot of first dates. Or maybe you get asked out on a lot of first dates but don't get asked out on a lot of second dates. Noticing patterns like these in ourselves can be really challenging and discouraging. I think it is important to remember what the end goal of dating is. It is not a popularity contest but an opportunity to get to know other people and to prepare for marriage.

The Brittany Example

I served my mission at the same time as a best friend of mine named Brittany. When we returned home from our missions, we both faced different challenges adjusting. She experienced ups and downs while dating. She found that she would get asked out by guys, and after two or three weeks they would stop calling. She explained to me that she had recognized this pattern and realized there was something she was doing to enable it. She was willing to take responsibility for her actions in the relationships, and she refused to push it onto the guys as "their problem."

I found her approach so humble and opposite to what many women in the world *and* the Church tend to do. Most of the time, we blame men for everything in dating that doesn't go our way, don't we? Brittany was not self-deprecating or blaming herself for failed relationships. She was simply recognizing that there was a pattern she wanted to change and she might be doing something that was making it harder to progress any further in these relationships. She explained to me that her plan was to pray and ask Heavenly Father for help to understand how she could be better. She was looking for ways to develop herself to be the best candidate for a future relationship. She got a master's degree, traveled, ran marathons, filled her schedule with social activities, served as the Relief Society president in her singles ward, and continued to date. She longed to someday be married and have kids. Then, one day she met a returned missionary named Scott. They met and the pattern in her dating life was broken! They dated for a few months, got engaged, married, and they had their first baby as he began his first year at medical school. Wow!

I was amazed as I watched Brittany humbly approach the scary, intimidating dating world. Rather than pushing the problem onto other people, she used her experience with dating as an opportunity to become more like the Savior. When asked if she had anything else to share with returned sister missionaries about dating, Brittany said this:

> "Sometimes we need to ask ourselves, what do I need to do to be a better candidate for marriage? We cannot change others, but we can change and improve ourselves. If you are noticing a pattern of failure in your dating experiences, you need to be honest with yourself that you may be the common denominator that is preventing relationships from progressing toward marriage. The Lord can and will help you, but remember that He cannot guide a car that is not moving. You must be doing your part. That does not mean just sitting around and praying fervently for Mr. Right. This life is an opportunity to learn and progress, and dating is not an exclusion!"

Rather than repeating the same patterns, Brittany actually made changes. She avoided the temptation to allow any negative dating situations to make her insecure or bitter. She moved forward and did not give up on her end goal, which for her was to be married in the temple.

Erin Schurtz SUPERSTAR

Erin Elton Schurtz has always been one of my role models. She works professionally as a social media strategist and is also the creator and executive producer of the online show *The Mormon Bachelor*. The show promotes the development of healthy, moral relationships. Originally from Santa Barbara, California, Erin served her mission in New Zealand. In October 2012, at the age of thirty-two, Erin married Seth, a Naval hunk, in the Los Angeles temple. When it comes to dating in the LDS singles scene, this sis knows it all. Listen up!

Q *Erin, you spent several years in the LDS single-adult world. What are some of the challenges you have identified?*

A There are several challenges in the single-adult LDS world:

First, single adults sometimes give up on their standards under pressure. It isn't easy to get into your late twenties and early thirties without a healthy romantic life—emotionally and physically. Singles become bitter as they watch their friends, loved ones, and even kids they used to babysit enter into healthy marriages that appear to be very loving. They never really lose their testimonies, but they find the commandments too difficult to endure, so they go on a different path.

Second, anxiety when making an eternal decision like marriage causes problems. The pressure of knowing whether someone is "the one" may manifest itself as stress and anxiety, which singles may interpret as being a "no" answer from the Lord. At first they feel like they are following the Spirit, but as the years roll by they notice that they continue to have failed relationship after relationship because they aren't letting themselves just enjoy the journey; they are too wrapped up in the end result.

Third, singles may just let themselves go because of disappointment in their dating lives. They stop caring about what they eat, how they dress, or personal hygiene. This doesn't do them any good when it comes to finding someone to date, but they lose hope in that happening so they just give into eating more, exercising less, and not putting effort into their physical appearance.

Q *Wow, so much great insight! With all these challenges, how did you find confidence in your dating life after returning home from your mission?*

A It took me awhile to find confidence in my dating life after my mission. I noticed that I wasn't really chasing after men, but as soon as one would show interest I would go overboard in nurturing him, and I would jump over the whole courtship period. I would find myself doing things for him that you only do in a more serious relationship—like cleaning his house, making every meal for him, buying him cute things that reminded me of him, etcetera. When every relationship would end with the guy not wanting to move forward, it confused me and made me feel like somehow I wasn't good enough.

Finally after so many of those failed relationships, I got fed up and decided that I wasn't going to settle anymore. I stopped paying for my own flights to visit guys out of town that had expressed interest in dating me. I stopped offering to pay for dates. I stopped doing so much for them too soon. I didn't change my personality at all; I didn't play hard to get. I just didn't start acting like an engaged or married woman; I acted like a woman who had many possible options ahead of me. It was amazing to me how my dating life changed after I changed my dating habits. Men started coming out of the woodwork and worked so hard to get me to date them. They started really courting me, and I started feeling like I was the valuable woman that I really was. When I acted like it, I was treated like it.

Q *Thank you so much for your honesty and for sharing what you found challenging. I think being honest with ourselves is half of the battle! You're happily married now. Do you have anything else to share with returned sister missionaries about dating?*

A Have fun dating and don't worry about being on a timetable or needing to get married right away. Find joy in the little things in life, develop your talents, explore your interests, meet new people, and date as much or as little as you want to! Overall, just have fun. Happiness shines through, and guys will see that and want it in their lives. Don't conform to what other people want to see in you—be who you are. Don't ever become bitter because a relationship doesn't work out—just look forward to meeting new people and discovering new friendships. Who knows what will come of them. Just enjoy them for what they are right now and look forward to the time when you meet someone who feels the same way about you and you can move forward in marriage. Until then, stop the pressure and enjoy where you are in life—no matter what your situation is, it can be great if you have the right attitude.

Work It, Girl!

With all that's at stake, how can dating be fun? Sister, have self-confidence in who you are. Please! You are a daughter of God. He loves you. Not only that, you are beautiful. You have recently spent a year and a half serving the Lord, and your spirit is radiant. People will see that in you. It is fun to date! Show people how rad you are and look for others who are equally awesome. When I met my husband, he told me that while he was on his mission he had decided he wanted to marry a returned sister missionary. All of the girls he had dated before me had served missions; he came home and dated mainly RSMs until he found the right one. Isn't that sweet? He felt like his mission had changed his life, and he wanted to share those experiences with a wife who could relate to what he had experienced. There are many boys who feel this way. Boys will be stupid to pass you up when you have such a great love for the Lord and His work. Be confident in who you are and what you have to offer. You are a catch—act like it.

Dating is fun when we are doing what is right. Keep the standards you were taught in *For the Strength of Youth*. Don't lower those standards, especially not now that you are an endowed, returned sister missionary.

How Do I Know If He's the One?

"Don't come home and find a guy who needs some love and encouragement. Don't be the girl who tries to save someone. Don't settle—marry up! You're worth it." —Anonymous

"Do not settle for dating guys you're not interested in just because they like you or they are good guys. How can God give you something better if you keep holding on to something that's not right?" —Sister Natalie D.

"Before meeting my husband, I wasn't sure what to do next. Before my mission, my plans were to get a higher education, serve a mission, and get married in the temple for eternity. I had control over the first two goals. The third was more difficult because I wasn't sure of the outcome: who I would marry, when we would marry, and, of course, having the power to make sure it would happen. You can't really plan getting married until you meet the right person, and that takes time and faith that it will happen one day (in this life or the next). But you can control getting married in the temple. Though I didn't have an idea of who or when, continuing to live the gospel standards helped me feel successful and confident that I would be happy and life would work out the way Heavenly Father planned for me." —Anonymous

As things progress in relationships, it is really important to stop and analyze a few important questions before moving on toward engagement and marriage. Because you usually only choose a spouse once, you want to make sure you are careful in your selection. You *do not* need to have conversations about these difficult topics with every boy you meet. You probably will only have them with one, or maybe with a few men that you date, depending on your experiences. But when the time is right, do not be shy about having a few serious conversations about important topics.

1. Will he be able to take me to the temple to be sealed?
2. Will he be a good father and example to our children?
3. Does he have similar views about money and spending habits?
4. Does he currently have or has he ever had a problem with pornography or same-sex gender attraction?
5. Does he have any financial debt?
6. Does he respect me as a daughter of God and treat me like one?
7. Am I physically attracted to him? (Like, do I want to kiss him a lot? The answer should be yes!)

If you can't honestly discuss these questions *together*, then this should be a concern. Take any concerns about these or any topics that might adversely affect your future marriage to your parents or leaders. Marriage can be wonderful, happy, joyful, and a dream come true. But an unhappy marriage is far more difficult and trying than being single. When you are single, it is sometimes hard to believe that! President Gordon B. Hinckley said:

"All of you presumably are without marriage partners. Many of you wish you were married. You think this would be the answer to all your problems. While a happy marriage should be the goal of every normal Latter-day Saint, let me assure you that for many who are married, life is miserable and filled with fears and anxiety. . . . I say that only to remind you that there are those who are married whose lives are extremely unhappy, and that you who are single and experience much of deep and consuming worry are not alone in your feelings."[6]

Keep the Lord on Your Side

Heavenly Father's hand is in all areas of your life. He wants to be a part of your dating life. Ask Him questions about dating in your prayers. When you receive an answer, get up and go and do! The good habits you create while dating will allow you to build lasting relationships that will follow you into your marriage. Get rid of habits like selfishness, insecurity, and laziness and become the type of person who would be successful in a marriage relationship. Dating is work, hard work! It requires sacrifice, humility, and faith. It can be discouraging and heart-wrenching when it does not go well, but it can also be a lot of fun. I would say that marriage is also work, hard work. The effort you put into successful dating relationships will be evident in your marriage.

Work hard to date and create relationships that progress. It doesn't mean that every boy you meet has to be your boyfriend, but it does mean that you should create good relationship patterns starting with every first date you have.

Take the Next Step

Is there an art to dating? I think there is, but it is different for everyone. In my guide to love, I have identified ways dating can be challenging. I recommend reading books that help you improve your relationship skills, asking roommates and family for honest advice, and taking time to talk to the Lord about your dating challenges. Use the reading suggestions, the self-analysis quiz, and the journal prompts to help you on your journey to finding your man!

Reading Suggestions

+ *For the Strength of Youth*
+ Dieter F. Uchtdorf. "The Reflection in the Water." CES Fireside, 1 Nov. 2009.
+ Gordon B. Hinckley. "A Conversation with Single Adults." *Ensign*, Mar. 1997.
+ Laura Schlessinger. *Dr. Laura, Stop Whining, Start Living*. New York: Harper Collins, 2008.
+ Henry B. Eyring. "O Remember, Remember." *Ensign*, Nov. 2007.
+ Earl C. Tingey. "The Simple Truths from Heaven: The Lord's Pattern." CES Fireside, 13 Jan. 2008.

Self-Analysis Quiz

Response Key

1 = never	4 = almost always
2 = sometimes	5 = always
3 = often	

Please use the key to honestly answer these statements:

_____ While on dates, I make conversation centered on others.

_____ I push too hard to progress the relationship, depriving the man of the ability to do the chasing.

_____ When appropriate, I show physical affection for someone I am dating.

_____ I respond kindly and timely when I am asked out.

_____ On occasion, I take the initiative to show someone I am dating that I care by planning an activity or being the first to reach out.

_____ I put myself in situations where people would be able to ask me out while at church, work, or school.

Journal Prompts

What more could I be doing to work on my dating habits? Is there something I am doing to hinder me from finding eternal marriage? What am I doing well in my dating life? What advice have I been given by loved ones that will help me be a well-rounded marriage candidate?

Chapter Six

DID THE SPIRIT BREAK UP WITH ME?

> "My mission taught me how to find the guidance of the Spirit in my day-to-day life. There is a saturation of the Spirit on your mission, and when I couldn't feel the presence or guidance of the Spirit, it usually had something to do with my lack of effort. So I could tweak my schedule to include more prayer, scripture study, or temple attendance, and I would find that guidance back in my life. What I missed that first year was the complete immersion into spiritual things. Coming home, the adjustment was learning to apply the spiritual learning to my everyday temporal life." —Sister Jamie P.

A FRIEND OF MINE STRUGGLED FOR MONTHS after her mission with some emotional ups and downs. We went out for breakfast one day, and I asked how she was doing. She said, "I feel like Jesus broke up with me. It's like we were together, going out every single day, and then He dumped me." I laughed so hard because I knew exactly what she meant! As missionaries, we felt connected to the Spirit in a way we never had before. After coming home, a lot of missionaries feel a void in their lives. The relationship with the Spirit that was once there at every street corner, scripture study, or lesson seems distant. This void, to whatever degree it is felt in your life, can be one of the hardest parts about readjusting to your new life.

I believe the change in our communication with the Spirit when we return does not mean the Lord has left us or "broken up with us." In this chapter we will talk about how to daily receive the guidance of the Spirit in our post-mission lives. This chapter mainly consists of the words of other returned sister missionaries and their experiences, but before we begin, let me just say this: I promise you that the Spirit has not left you.

God is still with you, Christ is still your Savior, and you still walk daily with the Spirit of the Holy Ghost—a gift God gave you because He loves you. Now, let's talk about how we can feel His love on a daily basis.

Trust in the Lord

"Trust in the Lord with all thine heart; and lean not unto thine own understanding. In all thy ways acknowledge him, and he shall direct thy paths. Be not wise in thine own eyes: fear the Lord, and depart from evil" (Proverbs 3:5–7).

I read this scripture differently after returning home from my mission. In the past I thought that this scripture refers to us consulting with the Lord on every decision in our lives and then waiting for His answer before moving forward. Because that is how it worked on a mission, right? Here's a mission scenario. You have a question: Which street should we knock? You say a prayer and immediately receive an answer: the left one. You proceed to the street, find a golden investigator, bring them eternal happiness, and go home at the end of the day knowing that you walked with the guidance of the Spirit. Here's a post-mission scenario: You have a huge life decision, you pray for weeks for an answer, you feel no answer or direction one way or another, and you feel incredibly frustrated and wonder what you're doing wrong. Why is this happening? Have you stopped feeling the guidance of the Spirit?

Since coming home from a mission, I have really come to understand what it means to "trust the Lord." I realize now that the act of involving the Lord and then moving forward in faith is *where* the trust comes in. Trusting in the Lord is trusting that He is aware of you, guiding you, and loving you even if that guidance feels differently than it did on your mission. Don't you just wish the Spirit would tell us what to do every minute of every day? I do! Go visit this person, take this class, move to this city, date this boy, take this job. It is so hard when making big decisions to consult with the Lord and not feel an answer from Him one way or another, especially when you have gotten used to feeling His direction so immediately as a missionary.

Sister, you need to trust the promptings you receive and trust that when you don't receive promptings that the Lord is proud of you and trusts you to direct the course of your life. Listen to the counsel of these two very wise returned sister missionaries:

"Coming home from my mission, I learned that the Lord was not going to tell me what to do. During my time as a full-time servant of His, I was told where to go, who my companion would be, and how I would carry out the work. His work. When I came home from my mission, I was waiting for this very detailed description of how to carry out the next phases of my life. What I learned was that God was not going to treat my life the same way He treats His missionary work. I was now free to choose for myself in every way. It was really hard to see value in things like going to school, dating, or working when my definition of 'work' was to spread the gospel to as many souls as possible. And so it went, day after day—me waiting for the Spirit to tell me what major to choose, who to date, and so on. He would not give me guidance until I would make an initial decision or step, and then He could help me to adjust my plan or better direct me to achieve a certain goal. I can say, though, that no matter how hard it ever was to come home, the Lord never left me alone." —Sister Marielle N.

"When it comes to feeling the guidance of the Spirit in day-to-day life, it is very important to remember Doctrine and Covenants 58:26: 'For behold, it is not meet that I should command in all things; for he that is compelled in all things, the same is a slothful and not a wise servant.' In the mission field I felt a lot of daily guidance because I had the full-time responsibility to find and teach those who were ready to receive the gospel. In my life now, I still share the gospel, but I have other responsibilities and decisions that don't always require strong spiritual promptings. I still feel the guidance of the Spirit, but I think some returned missionaries get confused because they don't feel strong spiritual guidance for where to go to school, what career path to take, who to marry, and so on. We need to take responsibility and make our own decisions, and we should not expect the Spirit to make decisions for us. Of course we need to stay close to the Lord, keep Heavenly Father involved in our lives through prayer, and continually seek the Spirit's guidance, but we need to make our own choices without waiting to be told what to do in every situation." —Sister Jessica S.

The Lord's Errand

Both Marielle and Jessica remind us that part of the reason we felt the guidance of the Spirit so strongly while serving a mission was because the guidance wasn't about us, it was about those we were serving. That's a humbling thought. Sometimes we associate missionary service with our own personal revelation, when in reality it is revelation the Lord gives us for others. Listen to this sister's thoughts on this:

> "It's hard because you are so used to having a special kind of spirit with you. When you come home, you may still be living righteously and thus have access to the gift of the Holy Ghost and daily guidance, but it is not as distinct. I have also found that as a missionary, you are often seeking guidance on behalf of others, which, for some reason, seems to come faster as compared to seeking answers for one's personal life. I have found that the promptings are much more subtle and come in other ways, such as through scripture, logical reasoning, or other people. As we mature in the gospel, the Lord trusts us more and does not feel the need to guide us in everything. There's not always one right answer. If you are living a good life, you will make good decisions."
> —Anonymous

A few years after returning home, I applied to get a master's degree in teaching English. The whole year I was applying, I felt a lack of peace. I would pray about my program and not receive an "answer," so I just continued to pursue the degree. After the semester started and I began taking classes toward my master's, I stumbled across an advertisement for a job online. The job was in a different field completely and was unlike anything I had ever before done. But for the first time in months, something felt peaceful and right. I realized that it was the Lord answering my prayers about what to do. Looking back, it all seems clear that the Lord was allowing me to just tackle these personal issues on my own. When the time was right and when things were needed, He stepped in and gave me an answer to prayers through peace. At the time, it felt like He hadn't heard my prayers.

On the other hand, I currently serve as the Young Women president in my ward. There will be nights when I wake up and think to text a certain girl or days when I know exactly what lesson I should teach next. These spiritual promptings for my girls seem to come often and quickly. I know that they come because they are on behalf of others rather than for myself. This experience gives me hope that, although I might not be receiving lightning bolt inspiration for myself throughout each day, when it is necessary God will bless others with that inspiration for me, just as He gives me the inspiration for the girls I currently serve. And when the time is right, He will intervene in our lives and direct us to help us find the right path.

Tell Me about It, SISTER

"Throughout my mission I had ample opportunity to refine my communication with God via the Holy Ghost. During my exit interview, I asked my mission president if I was going to lose the close companionship that had become as necessary to my everyday life as an arm, leg, vision, or the ability to hear. He told me as long as I was diligent in fulfilling my callings, reading scriptures, attending church, and praying that I would be just fine and the Holy Ghost would not leave me. The truth is, when I got home from my mission it was like the Holy Ghost and I were in a committed relationship, and then He dumped me. Post-mission I have always known God loved me on an intellectual level, but I have had a really hard time feeling it as regularly. The fluid communication I had loved so much and relied on slowed from a steady flow to what feels like a trickle. I don't think my mission president was wrong, and I'm not upset with him for saying what he did. In a way he was right. The Spirit hasn't left me. He goes where He's needed, and the life I live now apparently doesn't demand as much spiritual guidance as my mission life did. Regardless, I still feel an intense emptiness about this, aching at times. It's like giving someone all organic, nutrient-dense, power foods for eighteen months and then sending them back to fast food. I'm alive. I'm not hungry. My daily activities are more entertaining or fun than my mission, just like fast food seems to be more appealing, but I feel spiritually depleted often." — Sister Lindsay S.

You Are NOT ALONE

Many sisters have faced similar concerns. Of the over two hundred returned sister missionaries surveyed, almost half reported that in the first year home for their mission, they either "always," "most of the time," or "often" had difficulty feeling the guidance of the Spirit in their day-to-day lives.

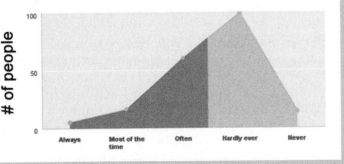

In the first year (1–12 months post-mission) of returning home from your mission, did you find it difficult to feel the guidance of the Spirit in your day-to-day life?

Melanie Burk SUPERSTAR

Melanie Monroe Burk is a designer, teacher, mother, and collector of happy. She is the owner of Melanie Burk Design. She designs logos, websites, décor, and children's toys. A total celeb graphic designer, she is sought after in her industry. Originally from Poway, California, Melanie and I went to high school together. Melanie served her mission in Rebeirao Preto, Brazil; is married to the most kind man alive, Dan; and has three darling daughters, Margaret, Adeline, and Samantha. To me, Melanie is the ultimate example of living a life that is directed by the Spirit. She has found a challenging balance of relying on the Lord and using her own intellect to make wise choices. In conversation, she will mention her scripture study, her temple attendance, or her goal setting. She is obviously working hard to be such a superstar.

Q *With so much to focus on, how were you able to keep the Spirit part of your daily life after returning from a mission?*

A I always joke that there is "the holy three": prayer, scripture study, and exercise. I have to make time for these every day or I have a hard time keeping the Spirit and staying positive and productive. It really does come down to those simple things. Another thing that really helped me was serving others. I still find that when I am having a hard day, all I need to do is serve someone, or call someone, or do something thoughtful. The smallest things can make the biggest differences.

Q *I love this! "Holy Three!" Perfect. In what ways did your mission change the way you live your day-to-day life?*

A I think it just changed my perspective. I learned so many things on my mission that help me every day, whether it be knowing how to serve others, teaching my children, serving my children, or loving others. Many of the lessons I learned on my mission help me in my daily struggles or challenges. More than anything, I feel like I know to be positive through it all and to maintain an eternal perspective, and I feel like that is a real blessing from serving a mission.

Q *As you gradually move away from being a full-time missionary to other roles, how do you continue to balance work, being a mom, and keeping your spiritual priorities straight?*

A Take it one day at a time! Like I mentioned earlier, I have to stick to the basics and put my priorities first. Like everyone, I have to make time for daily work—whether it be taking care of the house or running my business. I try to put my children and family first. When I take care of the most important things first, I find that everything else takes care of itself. Many days I don't get everything done I would like to, but I find that when I put the Lord and my family first, everything else takes care of itself.

Q *So smart. Melanie, do you have any other advice for returned sister missionaries you would like to share?*

A For me, serving a mission was wonderful, fulfilling, and life-changing. When I got home, my mission continued to shape the way that I lived, served, worked, and loved. It now reaches into every part of my life and is a pillar of strength for me.

It has been said that the best two years of your life are on your mission, and I would like to disagree. I believe that the best two years of your life should be the last two years of your life. I have found so much joy in my life post-mission. Being able to graduate in something I was passionate in was such a joy. Being able to get married was such a joy. Now being a mother is more challenging but more joyful than I could imagine. Life does just keep getting better—the challenges change and things are still tough at times, but overall, I love my life, and I wouldn't change it for any other time. So that is my advice—be happy where you are at and know that it just keeps getting better!

Chapter Seven

KEEPING THE FLAME ALIVE

"I always heard, 'You were on a mission—there's no way you are going to feel the way you did again.' However, I can't imagine a loving Father in Heaven wanting us to experience something so incredible for eighteen months and then take it away from us. If we put the effort into our daily spiritual necessities, we can still feel that guidance in our lives. A mission shouldn't be the spiritual peak of our entire lives but rather a training ground to learn how to receive revelation throughout the rest of our lives. Of course there are ups and downs, but I believe the spiritual high that we felt on a mission is not something we have to leave behind once we come home." —Anonymous

So, HOW DO WE DO IT? WE KNOW WE NEED TO trust the Lord and believe He is there, but we still need to do our part. Right? Of course! I will list a few things we can do when we come home to help us continue progressing spiritually and keep that missionary flame burning.

Stick to the Basics

Listen to these two wise sisters as they stress the importance of sticking to the basics when returning home:

"Don't lose the gifts you gained on your mission. Most sister missionaries gained a greater relationship with their Father in Heaven through service, scripture study, and personal prayer that helped them through the difficulties on the mission and helped them know what to do and who they were. That same relationship can help now that you are home, but it takes doing the same things you

73

did on your mission. It takes effort and can be hard some-times, but the results far outweigh the work. We taught people for eighteen months the importance of building a personal relationship with our Father in Heaven and what it takes to do that, and we cannot come home and think it doesn't apply to us. As we do the very things we taught our brothers and sisters, we will find it easier to transition home with all of its challenges." —Anonymous

"There is so much power in the basics. Missionaries so easily forget that when they come home. The same prin-ciples apply post-mission as on the mission. The same blessings are available if we continue to live the way we taught others to live." —Anonymous

Scripture Study

When I arrived in the MTC, I had no idea what it meant to "be a missionary." I was raised in a family of returned missionaries and attended mission prep at BYU, but my mission preparation involved a lot of shop-ping for cute clothes and the perfect suitcase to carry them in. The way I actually came to understand my purpose as a missionary was by studying *Preach My Gospel*, the scriptures, and my mission handbook. I would sug-gest that the same will be true when you return from your mission. Study the scriptures, your patriarchal blessing, and other Church doctrine for direction. Just as you came to know yourself as a missionary through the scriptures while you were serving, you will come to know who you are as a returned sister missionary as you study upon returning. Don't stop study-ing the scriptures; they will fill your life with purpose and peace. In them, you will find answers to your questions. Following are a few suggestions for successful post-mission study.

1. Commit to Study

When I was fourteen and at EFY, I decided I was going to study my scriptures every single day. I told myself it didn't matter how long, but every single day I was going to somehow read something or listen to something that brought the Spirit into my life. Now don't be too impressed, there have been many nights when at 2:00 in the morning I've gotten out my iPhone and read two or three verses with my eyes half open. But I know that if I miss a day or two it will be challenging to start up consistent study, so I don't let myself miss a day of scripture reading or some type of spiritual upliftment. I invite you to do the same thing. Will you do that? Will you make a goal to study your scriptures every single day and never miss? I promise you your life will be blessed more than you can imagine. I promise you will feel the presence of the Spirit. This sister feels the same way:

> "When I first got home, I stopped reading my scriptures. I remained active, but I dropped most of the habits of study and journal writing immediately. It wasn't because I didn't enjoy gospel studying; I think it was because I hadn't made up my mind to keep studying. Within the past couple of years, I've given myself up to sincere prayer and have desired to know God's will for me. Just this last week my family held a special fast, and I have felt the Spirit all week, even days after the fast."
> —Anonymous

2. Set a Time Each Day

Many returned missionaries struggle with the reality that their life just doesn't give them the time it once did to study the scriptures. Many have found success with this problem by breaking study into small chunks of time:

> "With kids and work, I just don't have that set-aside, one hour of study time, and it definitely makes it harder. I have to do scripture study several times throughout the day—in little chunks—to feel nourished and have the Spirit with me. Although I have the Spirit with me, I feel that more and more I have to make difficult choices and that the Lord is trusting me to make my own decisions."
> —Anonymous

Other sisters suggested setting a time each day to study:

> "Don't stop reading your scriptures. I was surprised by how easy it was to fall out of the habit of scripture reading when I returned home. I started school three weeks after I returned home, and as life became busier, I found myself reading less and less and some nights not at all. I became so busy that I didn't make time for scripture

study, and I felt the difference in my life. Even if you don't have time to study as long as you did on your mission, set a time aside each day to study the scriptures and other Church materials. Get in the habit of it right when you get home." —Anonymous

3. Spend Time in Meditation

In M. Catherine Thomas's book *Light in the Wilderness*, she refers to a "spiritual practice" that will help us come to know the Lord. She notes that meditation is pivotal to this practice. About meditation she says,

> For most of us, if we do not practice letting the mind down peacefully in a quiet time, we will not be able to do it amidst the busyness of daily life-which is where we need our spiritual presence most.... Therefore, in a set-apart, quiet time the mind can be stilled, perhaps just breathing for a bit as thoughts settle down, letting the silent, more subtle energies of one's spirit begin to rise. We invoke a deep calm and look to the Lord.[7]

I have never felt like I have needed a set-apart time for meditation more than I did when I returned from my mission. I found the Lord as I spent time meditating in the scriptures, in my own thoughts, and even in structured meditation like yoga. Bring meditation into your scripture study routine as you come home and allow yourself time to be still and feel God's love.

4. Keep a Journal

As missionaries, we take notes while we study and record impressions and the ideas that come to us for ourselves and our investigators. I often think about all of the impressions I have been given by the Spirit since my mission that I haven't written down. What am I thinking? I am always wishing I had a closer relationship with the Spirit and I am not taking the things seriously that I *am* directed in. Those impressions are sacred.

> "I kept a journal on my mission. As I have continued to do this, I can conscientiously look for the good in my life and see how Heavenly Father has blessed and guided me along life's journey." —Sister Amy C.

The key is to have a journal handy and to write down the impressions from the Spirit as they come while you are studying or throughout the day. My mission president told us that if we ever have questions, we just need to write them down and then attend a meeting or open our study materials, and through the Spirit we will find an answer. It totally works. Like magic! And by magic, I mean the Spirit. Try it! Today! It will help you avoid the frustrations Emily encountered:

> "I found it very frustrating trying to set aside the time to read and really study my scriptures. As a missionary, you always are reading with a purpose. You have investigators' needs in mind; you are looking for answers to the questions that you know people will ask you every day. It's like the feelings you have when studying a topic for a talk or a lesson. There is an urgency, and the Spirit guides you along. That urgency is there daily as a missionary, and I missed that so much. I felt my scripture study was very fruitless." —Sister Emily S.

Here's one last piece of advice from one of our sister friends:

> "You have spiritual experiences all of the time on a mission. The only way you can avoid spiritual experiences is if you are disobedient. After your mission, you have to create daily spiritual experiences by having meaningful scripture study and bearing your testimony often." —Anonymous

So, in other words, however you choose to study the scriptures, make it meaningful. If you are not currently getting anything out of your scripture study, think about ways to make it a powerful tool to bring the Spirit into your post-mission life.

Prayer

Don't stop praying with sincerity. If praying throughout the day was not a habit of yours before your mission, you might come home and easily allow this missionary principle to slide. Prayer has always been the way to bring peace and understanding into our lives, not just when we are missionaries. Besides, Jesus taught us that "whatsoever we shall ask the Father in my name, he will give it you" (John 16:23). Talk to the Lord about what you need, what you are thankful for, and what you are worried about. Other sisters found how important it was to continue to pray sincerely after a mission:

> "It is difficult to find your place back in the real world, which is why it is important to remember to rely on the Lord. I prayed for months to figure out what was next for me. The answer eventually came, and then I was on my way and things ran on from there." —Anonymous

> "It is important to remember that the only thing that changes after our tag comes off is that we don't hold the mantle of a missionary, and we no longer have a companion. We are the same people that we were on our missions, and we are entitled to the same inspiration that we received on our missions. It is easy on a mission to seek inspiration for others and to know how to help them because that is our purpose and calling. Now we have to seek inspiration for big decisions we have to make in our own personal lives. It is easier for Satan to tempt us and make us feel like we are inadequate. We have to recognize it, not panic, and go forward with faith, hope, and courage. I know the Lord wants to help us. It depends on us—we need to continue to study the scriptures, pray regularly, and be engaged in our Church callings. As we are living the commandments, we are entitled to the direction of the Spirit in our lives." —Sister Kimberly W.

Temple

Other sisters shared advice on attending the temple to keep the Spirit in our lives:

> "Be patient. Try to go to the temple often. Keep up the good habits and routines you learned on your mission as much as possible. Don't expect things to be the same as before or during your mission. Move forward with faith. Things get easier." —Anonymous

"Go to the temple often, at least weekly or monthly. Do the little things and don't lose your light. Just continue to follow the Lord, and it will all be well." —Anonymous

Peer Group

Last, it is important to note that our peer groups will greatly influence our choices as returned sister missionaries. Place yourself in situations that make it easy to make good choices and feel the love of the Lord.

I have watched close friends and family come home from missions and not only stop pursuing spiritual guidance but also allow the media or a peer group to guide their actions. In one instance, it was as if I saw the Spirit start to leak out of the person only to be filled with doubt, confusion, fear, and unhappiness. The change was so quick and noticeable that it was almost like each dirty song, offensive movie, and Internet site took the direction of the world and replaced the direction of the love of God. After watching this person—whom I dearly love—make such a harsh transition, I realized that having the direction of the Spirit often has much to do with what we do but even more what we *don't* do. Choose peer groups and places that will allow you to be filled with good. Don't let your mind be filled with garbage—you know what I'm talking about.

The Best Eighteen Months

I promise you that your mission was not the best eighteen months of your life. Spiritually, you still have so much to feel and learn from your Heavenly Father. I always find it interesting when listening to talks in church how often people share experiences from their missions. I *love* mission experiences. I love how strongly they bring the Spirit. But sometimes I wonder if the reason we share mission stories so often is because those are our only experiences with the Spirit. Have you ever thought about that? If you had to give a talk on prayer, temple attendance, or fasting, would you have experiences from the life you are living today? If the only spiritual experiences we can think to share happened while on our missions, then we aren't spending enough time seeking the guidance of the Spirit. We will feel distance from the Lord when we aren't having daily experiences with Him. Just like we miss our friends, siblings, and parents when we aren't with them, we will miss the Spirit if we don't spend time inviting Him into our lives. Gradually our connection with spiritual things will diminish, and it will be more challenging to feel how strongly the Lord loves us.

It does not matter where we currently are spiritually. Elder Jeffrey R. Holland teaches, "The size of your faith or the degree of your knowledge is not the issue—it is the integrity you demonstrate toward the faith you do have and the truth you already know."[8] Continue to be true to the spirit you felt during your missionary service, and find ways to live with that spirit daily as you return.

Reading Suggestions

+ Jeffrey R. Holland. "Lord, I Believe." *Ensign*, May 2013.
+ L. Tom Perry. "The Returned Missionary." *Ensign*, Nov. 2001.
+ *Preach My Gospel*, chapter 4.
+ Alma 5
+ M. Catherine Thomas. *Light in the Wilderness: Explorations in the Spiritual Life*, Salt Lake City: Digital Legend, 2010.

Self-Analysis Quiz

Response Key

1 = never   4 = almost always
2 = sometimes   5 = always
3 = often

Please use the key to honestly answer these statements:

_____ I trust that the Lord is aware of who I am and what my needs are.
_____ I have purposeful daily scripture study.
_____ I pray morning and night.
_____ I make sacrifices to regularly attend the temple.
_____ I regularly repent and look to be better.
_____ I work hard to not allow negative influences to affect me spiritually.

Journal Prompts

How have I recently felt the love of the Lord? What more could I be doing to invite the Spirit into my life? What questions do I have about my life or those I love that I need help answering?

Chapter Eight

CALLED TO SERVE ... STILL!

"If you're not a full-time missionary with a missionary badge pinned on your coat, now is the time to paint one on your heart—painted, as Paul said, 'not with ink, but with the Spirit of the living God.' And returned missionaries, find your old missionary tag. Don't wear it, but put it where you can see it. The Lord needs you now more than ever to be an instrument in His hands. All of us have a contribution to make to this miracle."[9] —Neil A. Anderson

MY FIRST CALLING AFTER MY MISSION WAS IN A Relief Society presidency at BYU. When I was called, the Relief Society president told me they had a really hard time getting people to stay for Relief Society and come to activities. "Well," I thought, "little does she know who I am! I am Sister Faulkner, freshly returned sister missionary!" I was just positive that a little faith and RSM zeal could fix all of this in a snap.

As a counselor, I was over enrichment, so I invited the girls on the enrichment committee over to my house. I explained to them that we should set a goal for how many people we wanted to have at our upcoming activity. It was just like weekly planning—so fun! "It's simple," I said. "We just to need set a goal, and then we need to fast, pray, and work as hard as we can to get this number of girls to the activity. The Lord will do the rest." I looked up to see if the committee had caught the vision, but all I was catching was a lot of blank stares. I wasn't quite getting the enthusiasm I had hoped for. I was so excited about my idea and thought that obviously they would jump on the idea to exercise their faith over a Thursday night Relief Society social. So I know you're wondering . . . what happened? How many girls came to enrichment that month? I think there were ten. It wasn't exactly the loaves and fishes miracle I'd hoped for. This was the first time I realized that post-mission Church service would be slightly different than my experience in the field.

Don't be discouraged if you have one or two experiences like this. Although you have been released from your full-time missionary calling, you are still called to serve in many other capacities in the Church. The trick is not to lose your missionary zeal but learn how to apply it in a new setting! For example, I am currently the Young Women president in my ward. Early on in my time serving, the missionaries came over and said they wanted to set some baptismal goals for my auxiliary. We sat down, made a list of names, and covered who we felt were potential baptismal candidates. Later that week I met with my presidency, and together we set goals for this list of investigators I had made with the missionaries. It was such a positive, familiar experience and something I would not have clearly understood how to do if I hadn't served a mission. My counselors were really receptive, and we even planned fasts with the young women for one of our investigators. I still had my enthusiasm for missionary work, but I took my aggressive approach down just a notch, and my counselors caught the vision and got excited.

My mission has blessed my Church service and my marriage, and it has made me a more confident employee, mother, and friend. Occasionally people might be taken aback by your RSM zeal—and I think that is just fine. You need to remember that if the people you serve with don't always catch your vision, that's okay. It is not their vision—it is yours. Your calling is an opportunity to exercise *your* faith. Church service is about perfecting our lives to be better servants to those around us, and it is not dependent upon the ward you are in, how you feel others around you are performing their service, what calling you have, or how busy you are. Our service in the Church is a way for us to show Heavenly Father that we love Him and that we want to consecrate our lives to Him. Some experiences will be very rewarding, and some (like the enrichment story) will be more challenging and will not always feel successful. Magnifying our callings has to do with growing personally, showing love like the Savior would, and demonstrating faith.

Sharing the Love

Preach My Gospel tells us, "Wherever you are assigned to serve, remember that the Lord has 'suffered you to come unto this place.'"[10] I believe that when you return home, this principle still applies. Wherever you currently are is where you are called to lift. When you serve a mission, you learn the skills involved in doing missionary work. A lot of people in the Church, especially sisters, are uncomfortable talking about principles of the gospel with friends and family members of other faiths because they have never had practice doing it. If you stop sharing the gospel when you come home, you will become one of these people—don't let that happen! Pray for missionary opportunities in your local area; pray to be able to continue to be a missionary in your role as a member. It can be tricky to find that balance at first, but it will come over time. Here's how Andrea found the balance:

> "When I came home, I had a hard time knowing my role as a member missionary. I had good goals, but I felt stressed out about it. With time I realized you have a different relationship with the Lord when you are serving Him full time. I would wonder, 'Am I being prideful to want these member missionary experiences?' I did have the opportunity to have cool experiences. One thing that helped me find a balance was getting a calling. I was in the Relief Society presidency and then eventually called as the president. I loved contacting people who were less active and taking my visiting teaching really seriously." —Sister Andrea P.

Jessica Downs SUPERSTAR

Jessica Mortenson Downs and I were roommates in Provo after our missions. She served her mission Spanish-speaking in New York City, is a mom to Booker and Eloise, and teaches writing at a community college in Colorado. Somehow Jessica manages to be an intensely spiritual person without ever coming off as "churchy." On top of that, she is a total babe without even trying! When I grow up I want to be as good of a Christian as she is. Jessica is one wise woman.

Q *Jessica, how did your mission shape the way you currently serve in the Church?*

A On a mission, we're exposed to a lot of leadership and a lot of members. I can still think of a number of people who were my "favorites," and they were not necessarily the ones who so kindly contributed to my excessive sister missionary weight gain. They were the ones I could count on to do just a little extra. I don't mean that they made things prettier with doilies or clever handouts, but that they always welcomed new people to church or to the classes they were teaching or to their homes. They were kind and willing and genuine. Seeing how helpful and significant those small efforts were has made a difference in the way I try to serve in my ward now, both inside and outside of my calling. I find myself still watching for new people to come in through the chapel doors. I know it counts to say hello or to offer some of my time to someone. It's simple, but it makes a real difference.

Q *I love this! It is so true. It is those small efforts that make the difference. How has your mission made you more capable of helping the local missionary effort?*

A This has been a very clumsy, often graceless process but I think it is leveling out to something sustainable, not only for me, but for people I share the gospel with. In the first few months after my mission, I handed out countless copies of the Book of Mormon to people on airplanes and to neighbors—few of whom (if any) received them very well. I was a normal person trying to be a New York City missionary, always ready to share a message. But it turns out, there are differences in the way the gospel is shared in a city of 8 million people, where I am only a temporary force, and in my home, where I am permanent and my relationships have time to develop.

Since then, my efforts have been a little more tempered in that I'm not quite so eager to say, "This message will change your life for good forever!"

One thing that hasn't completely changed, however, is my awareness. I try to be aware, like I was as a missionary, and look for ways to offer some of the peace of the gospel to the people I meet and spend time with. I learned something very valuable from the people of Texas in the three years I lived there after my mission: It is okay to have my faith be a normal part of my everyday conversation with others. I was told all the time, "Have a blessed day!" When I asked people about their weekends, Sunday school or the preacher's sermon often came up in the same report of some good barbecue or a good show they saw Saturday night. There was not a distinction between the fun they had and the faith they held.

I am trying to adopt the same perspective instead of "I'm a missionary, I have this message." I can be a good friend. I can offer service. I can set up playdates for my little boy and his neighborhood buddies. And I can share the gospel in small, regular doses because now I have the time, which is not limited to whether a person says "yes" or "no" on the doorstep, which, really, is so much better.

Q *Let's hear it for Texas! Do you have anything else to share with returned sister missionaries? Give us your wisdom, sister!*

A As sister missionaries, we were encouraged to forget ourselves and get to work. And we do: We go on our missions, we focus on the people on our missions, and we forget everything. And then we come back home and still can't remember! We can't remember how to dress ourselves outside of a long skirt and a button-up blouse. We can't remember how to have conversations with boys that don't involve someone we taught on our missions. We can't remember how to be funny in a way that people other than missionaries will laugh at, or how to live a life without two-plus hours of daily scripture study. But what we forget is replaced with something very good. Something that should be treasured. And gradually, the missionary life will meld with the new life in a balanced, beautiful way. And that old forgotten stuff of the old forgotten self will not be missed. The first little while is hard and uncomfortable because it is hard to find people who value all that new stuff as much as you do. Sometimes you might want to retreat. There are still things, five years later, that are hard for me. But so much (maybe all) of my very good life can be traced back to what I did as a missionary—and what I didn't forget when I came home.

Visiting Teachers Are Missionaries Too!

One of the greatest ways to keep the missionary fire burning is to get involved as a visiting teacher. You can take a missionary approach to this very fundamental assignment with great results. Rose says:

"Get involved as soon as possible! Ask for a calling, get a job, go back to school, etcetera. Spend every moment you have once you get home working on your next steps. Keep serving, just remember that your role as a member missionary will be different than a full-time missionary. I love the quote by President Harold B. Lee: 'Missionary work is but home teaching to those who are not now members of the Church, and home teaching is nothing more or less than missionary work to Church members.'[11] The sisters you visit teach have been assigned to you by the revelation of the Spirit to your Relief Society president. They need you." —Sister Rose K.

Make a goal never to miss contacting those you visit teach each month—ever! As time rolls on and your life becomes increasingly busy, you will find that making time to do your visiting teaching will be difficult if it isn't a top priority. But if you are diligent and consistent about it, you will also find that there is not a more inspired program in the Church. Pray for the sisters you visit, ask the Lord to help you understand their needs, be their friend, and watch miracles happen.

After returning home from my mission, getting married, enrolling in school, and working, I felt pretty overwhelmed. How could I possibly find success in each of these roles all at the same time? After months of feeling like I was drowning in every area, I decided to establish one goal for Church service for my *whole* life. Just one! Are you ready? Here it is: Be a good visiting teacher. This encompasses the way I view the gospel, my local ward, and my commitment to be open to service. I figure if I am always reaching out to the sisters I visit teach, I will always have a service-oriented mentality, be close to my ward family, and, as a result, be close to the Lord.

Being a good visiting teacher does not mean you spend hours with those you visit teach each month. It means you are a part of their lives to the point that you know their needs and have a relationship that makes it comfortable to serve them appropriately. Provide friendship, service, and love. If you're feeling lost and need to give service, think about how you can improve your relationship with those you have been assigned to visit teach. This is the perfect place to start.

Love the Missionaries

As a returned sister missionary, I have also found that I have a unique opportunity to influence other missionaries. Siblings, friends, and ward members who serve missions all need letters, so write the missionaries! Talk to them about your experience serving and about the passages in the scriptures and *Preach My Gospel* that changed your life. Send them encouraging letters that will help them stay focused on their purpose. If I hadn't been a missionary, I wouldn't have known how important thoughtful, inspiring letters are. They help missionaries feel encouragement from home and more commitment to their work. I remember having family home evening as a little girl with our family and writing the missionaries from our ward. My mom and dad would write each of the elders and sisters inspiring letters, filled with examples of faith from their missions and the scriptures. They sent such great uplifting advice, and what a blessing it was to those sweet missionaries.

In addition, the missionaries in your own area need love and encouragement. Sometimes it is tempting to look at them and wonder why they aren't doing more. But judgment is *not* what they need. If you think about the members who blessed you on your mission, I am sure it was because they loved you and gave you strength through kind words and appropriate dinner appointments! Instead of telling the local missionaries what they should be doing, ask the missionaries about their investigators, how you can help progress the work in your area, and what they stand in need of right now. Then be there for them!

Continue to Convert Your Converts

While I was serving in a singles ward on my mission, a girl named Jen was introduced to us who was interested in the Church. We taught Jen a first lesson and invited her to be baptized. After that she stopped taking the lessons, but we would still call her often. (Read: Every single day!) I returned to Nauvoo to finish my missionary service, and Jen and I kept in contact through the mail for the remainder of my mission. Guess what? She started meeting with the missionaries again and decided to be baptized. When I returned home from my mission, she came to see me while I was at school in Provo. Over the next few years, we stayed in touch on Facebook, would text occasionally, and even chat on the phone. Two years after I had been home, Jen invited me to come to Colorado to be her escort when she was married in the Denver temple. She met a darling guy in the singles ward, and they are so in love. She now reads my blog and will leave comments suggesting her favorite Church talks, and occasionally I will just cry thinking about how happy it makes me to be able to stay in touch with her. Being in the temple with Jen on her wedding day was one of the greatest joys of my life, and I am so happy we have continued our friendship since my mission.

President Gordon B. Hinckley said, "You missionaries . . . are part of this responsibility of binding your converts to the Church. You may not be able to continue to visit them. But you can write to them occasionally and give them encouragement. . . . When you go home do not forget them. At all times live worthy of their trust. Write to them occasionally, assuring them of your love."[12]

Aren't we lucky to live during a time when we can email, Instagram, and Facebook people all over the world? Let's not neglect these valuable tools to help us continue to influence the people we were blessed to serve.

Hastening the Work of Salvation

Sister, are you sad that you are no longer a full-time missionary? Well, I have good news for you! Never before in the Church have the prophets and apostles been so adamant about the need for members to be member missionaries. The worldwide training "Hastening the Work of Salvation" is a great place to start as you transition from a full-time missionary to member missionary. Being a member missionary, in my experience, is even more challenging and rewarding than being a full-time missionary. So, if you ever start to miss your role as a servant of the Lord, don't be discouraged; nothing has changed. You are still in fact called to serve!

Chapter Nine

TAKING THE FOCUS OF OF YOU

"It's important to take the fire you had on your mission and apply it to the new ward you are in. Befriend everyone and make sure everyone is progressing, including yourself. You can easily throw yourself into a new calling and then spend the rest of your time being normal." —Sister Kelly R.

The Welcome Wagon

ONCE WORKED IN AN OFFICE WITH EIGHTY WOMEN. You can imagine the cliques, gossiping, and competition that went on. My first few months, I was totally intimidated and felt super worried about being included. A few months into my time at the office, a new girl was hired on my team named Stephanie. Stephanie came in and did the opposite of what the rest of us had done when hired. Every day she looked for people who looked lost or lonely and reached out to them. She planned lunches, work outings, and threw people birthday parties. She quickly became the most loved person in the office because she made her first few months about others and not about herself. A year later we asked Stephanie how she was so good at "being new." She said she had moved a lot when she was first married and decided that instead of always being the new girl waiting for someone to befriend her, she would be the welcome wagon and invite anyone who looked lonely to join. She looked for ways to serve others instead of just sitting around thinking about herself. This gave her purpose and friends wherever she went. What a genius idea, Stephanie!

As a returned sister missionary, you will be placed in many situations similar to my office job. Will you reach out to others as the welcome wagon and love and serve them, or will you act like me and spend time worrying about other people reaching out to you? I promise that your service in whatever situation you find yourself will bless your life more than you can imagine. In many ways, service will save you from any sadness or loneliness you might feel when you return. In this chapter, we will discuss a few of the ways you can be a welcome wagon in whatever situation you are placed in as a returned sister missionary. All aboard! (Or whatever you say for wagons . . .)

Every Calling Counts

No matter what stage of life you are in, you should always be investing time in your calling. A few years ago I moved to a new ward and was called to be the nursery leader of eighteen toddlers. Nursery? I had never even stepped foot in the nursery. I was not excited at first for the challenge, but I accepted and went in with a so-so attitude. My ever-wise mother prompted me to study the nursery manual. Let me just tell you, it is life changing! As I read the manual, prepared my lessons, and fulfilled my calling, I came to know the Savior better. The lessons I taught to those distracted two-year-olds every Sunday were just as important as the lessons I had taught investigators on my mission.

Be patient, loving, and dedicated in your calling, whatever it is. Use the skills and work habits you learned on your mission to serve in your local ward and stake. Your goal should be to make every program you serve in better. Just like you would want to leave any area you served in as a missionary better, think of your calling the same way. It might be helpful to fill in the following blank: When I was a missionary, I loved the way _____ served. Think of a ward mission leader, bishop, Relief Society president, or teacher who made your life as a missionary easier because they were always prepared and you could count on them for your investigators. Have you made yourself into one of those people in your current ward or branch? If not, what do you need to do to become that person?

You Are NOT ALONE

Of over two hundred returned sister missionaries interviewed, more than one-third felt that "always," "most of the time," or "often" there was not a place for them in their home ward after they returned. When you are a missionary, you are like a mini-celebrity in your local ward or branch. Everyone greets you and is involved in your experience each Sunday. Returning home and going to church as a civilian can be surprisingly lonely. You might feel like you are lost or not needed like you once were. Obviously a lot of sisters have felt this way. Take Krystal's advice:

"I used to wonder why missionaries went inactive, but now I clearly see how that can happen. It is hard to go to church sometimes after being home. I often feel overlooked in my ward. I do my part to reach out and befriend others. I am active each week. I volunteer and comment in lessons. I teach Sunday school. I feel like I'm trying to do my part to make the ward stronger and more friendly, but even after living in the ward now for a year and half, the Relief Society president still asks me if I am new. It is frustrating. I just continually remind myself that the gospel is true no matter what the people do. I can only pray that it will get better. I won't give up in the spiritual battle and fall into inactivity. I don't want the adversary to drag me down. I need the Lord to guide my life. I can't be complacent. Pray every day! Study with all your heart daily! Don't forget the feelings of the sweet Spirit." —Sister Krystal M.

Rachel also found this to be true. Although she says it wasn't easy, she found that reaching out to others made her transition easier:

"I tried to get involved in my student ward and in callings. My bishop asked me to befriend another sister missionary that had gotten home a few months after I had. He said she was having a hard time being home. He wanted me to help encourage her to go to FHE, activities, and so on. I took the request seriously and really tried to reach out to her, knowing how she was feeling. We became fast friends, and in the process of inviting her to activities, it helped me have a friend and someone to lean on as well. I'm sure his request was to make sure I went to activities and stayed involved as well. I attended institute classes and spoke with the high counselors during their visits on Sundays to different wards. I tried to encourage others in missionary work and tried to keep up my studying and temple attendance and follow the counsel of my mission president. It wasn't easy and took a lot of prayer. Sometimes I felt alone, but in helping others and finding positive ways to fill my time and serve, I found I was happiest." —Sister Rachel P.

Service Any Time, Any Place

When I returned home from my mission, I really wanted to teach the gospel and find opportunities to share it. At the time, I wanted to do those things in the same way I had done while I was a missionary. I wanted to teach lessons and contact and commit people. I look back and wonder how much more success I would have had if I had come home and found ways to serve others in the ways *they* needed. Most people aren't ready for the missionary discussions or even a gospel conversation. Maybe your family needs you to tackle a project around the house or needs some extra help babysitting. Maybe your local ward needs help with a big activity they are planning or a Primary class they don't have a teacher for. Below are three examples of how returned sister missionaries found ways to serve after returning that enriched their lives.

1. Service through Employment

"I made a place for myself where I could help other people. Upon returning home, I was offered a position as a resident director that I felt impressed to take, even though I would have rather lived off campus with my friends. I will forever be glad I followed the impression to serve the girls I lived with in that way. It truly was a continuation of the spirit of service of my mission, especially when I was called to be Relief Society president for that same group of girls. As we follow the Spirit, we can find opportunities to serve over and over again." —Sister Mara H.

2. Worldwide Humanitarian Service

"I have always thought of service in a church context (magnify my callings, do my visiting teaching, be inspired as to who needs my help that day, be kind to others, and so on), but my eyes have been opened to the endless needs of those who live in poverty and the opportunities that are available to serve outside of the Church. There's a whole world out there of people who give their lives in serving those in need and of life beyond the first world that needs us." —Sister Lorraine G.

3. Local Community Volunteer Work

"On my mission it was 24-7 about the Lord and sharing the gospel with other people. When I came home I had two weeks, and then I was right back in school. All of a sudden, it was 24-7 about me, and I had a hard time dealing with that. I felt really useless and selfish because I wasn't helping people all of the time. But we're not expected to live like missionaries our entire lives. We have to take time to do things for ourselves. I found that going to the temple weekly and volunteering at Friday's Kids Respite (a non-profit organization in Utah Valley that helps families of kids with disabilities) really helped me not to feel so selfish. It was time that I could do things for other people. Weekly service really helped me to feel grounded." —Sister Sarah M.

Finding meaningful opportunities to give of ourselves to others will, like Sarah said, "make us feel grounded." As you pray and look for opportunities to serve people every single day in the ways *they* need, you will feel directed to those who need you now. This is how you will find joy.

Tell Me about It, SISTER

66 As regular life took over after my mission (school, work, marriage, and children) I slowly began to slip away from the everyday things I needed to be doing to have the Spirit with me. I couldn't seem to make time for personal prayer and scripture study. I was

still actively participating in church and had a testimony, but I felt myself hardening and slowly slipping away from feeling as close to my Heavenly Father. I began to long for my mission and wish that I could feel the same now as I did then. I thought I missed it just because during my mission I only had one responsibility—teaching the gospel—instead of all of the million things we try and do in one day. But that wasn't it. What I missed was the way I felt. What I felt was the constant companionship of the Holy Ghost and a closeness with the Lord.

"I made a resolution to feel closer to the Lord. I asked my dad for a blessing. Not too long afterward, I was called to be the Primary president. The Lord wanted me to be close to Him too. This calling has forced me to rely on my Heavenly Father much the same way I did as a missionary. Sitting in ward council meetings talking about ways we can help others come unto Christ has taught me that I can feel the same way now as I did on my mission. I am sad it took so long for me to see it when really I knew it all along. Even when I don't have this calling, I now know what I can do. Personal prayer and scripture study first of all, and then really serving, praying, and fasting for those around me." —Sister Stephanie W.

Judge Not

Many of the survey participants who contributed to this book mentioned the importance of not judging others. I include this in the chapter on service because I believe an open heart and mind can be the most challenging and most Christlike form of service. I found the responses of the sisters about judging others so insightful. In retrospect, many wished they had been less quick to judge the actions of those around them when returning home.

"I had a personal mantra when I got home: Everybody sins differently. This helped me avoid judging other people and softened the blow when I felt bad that I wasn't being my ideal returned missionary self. After several months of being home and much effort to understand my mantra, I felt I had regained more charity for the people around me, which was something I felt strongly while being a missionary." —Sister Mandi B.

Shortly after my mission, I was working at the MTC, and I was unbelievably frustrated with my district. I felt like they weren't living up to their potential. A dear friend and fellow teacher listened to my frustrations and said, "In their hearts and minds, these missionaries are doing the very best they know how. It might not be the best you've ever seen, but it is the best for them." I always think about that experience in my service with others at church. Most of the time people are doing the best they know how, even if we feel like it isn't enough. We have no idea what other variables in their lives are causing them to act a certain way. Buddha said, "Expect nothing." Setting expectations, for ourselves and others, at an unreasonable level is exhausting and discouraging. It makes it really difficult to see the good in others and it makes it tiring for us to try to keep up with these unrealistic standards. Plus, there is that whole issue with us having to be accountable for how we judge others. Remember?

"Judge not, and ye shall not be judged: condemn not, and ye shall not be condemned: forgive, and ye shall be forgiven" (Luke 6:37).

"See that ye do not judge wrongfully; for with that same judgment which ye judge ye shall also be judged" (Moroni 7:18).

Yikes. After returning home from an experience when 100 percent of your time was devoted to studying and living the gospel, it can be extremely challenging not to wonder why other people have lost the vision. You might look at your family and think, "What is the matter with you?" I love how these two sisters below teach us how they were able to avoid passing judgment with their families:

"I tried to be an active member of my family by listening more and not trying to fix them. I found after returning from my mission that I had a kind of arrogance, that I was better than others because I was so close to the Spirit for a year and a half. As I tried to listen more and support my family members, I was happier. It took time to find confidence and success as a returned sister missionary. It also took effort, faith, patience, prayer, and using my time wisely to find the comfort and happiness I desired." —Anonymous

"It took a while for me to learn how to be a member missionary and not a full-time missionary. Not being a full-time missionary was really hard for me at first. I came home to a partially active family and began acting like their missionary. Needless to say, that did not go over well. As a member missionary, my job was not to call my family to repentance, but rather to love them, be an example, and bear my testimony of important gospel truths." —Anonymous

If we really want to serve others, we will avoid the tendency to judge them. As you take a minute to consider how you come across to other individuals, you will be able to find the balance of being true to yourself while not judging. I have faith that if anyone can achieve this difficult balance, it's you!

I Love to Have the Last Word!

Sister, here is one last word about service: Whatever is going on in your life, whatever you are experiencing that is difficult or confusing or heartbreaking, service will always be a good idea. If we are serving those around us, lifting up our ward family, and reaching out to those we visit teach, we will always be able to think, "I am doing something the Lord is proud of." I second-guess a lot of things I do in my life. Do you? Little things like "Should we have lasagna or chicken?" or "Should we get a blue or red comforter?" But then there are the big things that I wonder about, such as "Where should we live?" Maybe you wonder, as I do sometimes, "Is the Lord proud of me?" I am glad to have a few things in my life that I never have to second-guess, and service is one of those. I can promise you that if you serve sincerely, you will never have to wonder if it was the right thing to do. I always know that it is good and right to serve, and when it is done with a willing heart and sincere intention, I will possibly make a difference in the life of someone else, and I will most definitely see my life change as well.

The transition home from a mission will be like any big change in your life; it will probably include some long days and lonely nights. There will be times when you desperately miss being a full-time missionary. Serving others, especially in the Church, will keep you close to the Lord, take the focus off of you, and put it back where it was on your mission—on the Savior! Be the welcome wagon like Stephanie, don't judge others, and serve in your ward and community. Service will heal your heart with His redeeming power, and there is no greater feeling in the world. Don't miss this opportunity for service that will help you come home and bring all of the goodness of being a missionary into your home life. It's too good!

Reading Suggestions

+ Alma 9:28; James 1:22, 27; Mosiah 2

+ Clayton Christensen. *The Power of Everyday Missionaries*. Salt Lake City: Deseret Book, 2013.

+ Dieter Uchtdorf. "Lift Where You Stand." *Ensign*, Nov. 2008.

+ M. Russell Ballard. "Finding Joy through Loving Service." *Ensign*, May 2011.

+ *Preach My Gospel*, chapter 9.

· *Handbook 2: Administering the Church* (The most inspiring thing you can do for your calling is to read the handbook associated with your assignment!)

+ www.lds.org (search "Hastening the Work of Salvation")

Self-Analysis Quiz

Response Key

1 = never	4 = almost always
2 = sometimes	5 = always
3 = often	

Please use the key to honestly answer these statements:

_____ I am involved in my local ward.

_____ I prayerfully fulfill my calling.

_____ I regularly pray for missionary opportunities.

_____ I make efforts to assist the local missionaries with missionary work.

_____ I am the type of visiting teacher who can be relied on.

_____ I keep in touch with converts from my mission and lift and inspire them.

_____ I resist the urge to judge those around me.

_____ When placed in new situations, I reach out to others.

Journal Prompts

What else can I do to bless the lives of the people I have been called to serve? What keeps me from being a better visiting teacher? What do the sisters I visit teach need right now? How can I assist the local missionaries with missionary work? What would serving in a way that would satisfy the Lord look like to me?

_____

_____

_____

_____

_____

_____

_____

_____

_____

_____

_____

_____

_____

_____

_____

_____

_____

_____

_____

_____

_____

_____

_____

Chapter Ten

BUMPS IN THE ROAD

"As a missionary, it is not hard to determine your identity. You are wearing a badge that tells you if you ever do forget. When returning home, you need to reconcile the old you and the new you who has a load of experiences that do not always fit into civilian living. Therefore, you combine the old you and the missionary you to create a new returned missionary you. We are always changing and having new experiences. There is one part that never changes—we are children of God. That is why the gospel of Jesus Christ has to always be our rock and foundation. If you understand that and repeat the Young Women motto every once in a while, you will never be completely lost." —Sister Ashley S.

HAVE YOU EVER BEEN MOUNTAIN BIKING? THE first time I went mountain biking, my husband, Brian, taught me the two cardinal rules to getting down the mountain: Sit back, and look where you want to go. What? That's it? Seems too easy right? It's hard to trust these simple mantras when you are sliding down a rocky hill feeling slightly (or in my case, really) out of control. I have always loved cycling, but I am a total wuss and find most mountain biking trails absolutely terrifying. But just as Brian warned, I have found that the only times I have fallen is when I have looked down at the obstacle just ahead of me. When I look down, I start to question my capability as a biker, and before I can look back up to move forward, I end up on the ground, on a rock, covered in the dirt I was trying to get past. Occasionally while we are out riding and are approaching an obstacle, my husband will call back to me, "Look where you want to go!" because he knows I am terrified and I need that reminder.

Coming home from a mission can feel a little like sliding down a dirt hill. At times you feel out of control, and there are a lot of bumps and scary obstacles that might be uncomfortable and terrifying. So today I am going to give you the same advice: "Sit back, and look where you want to go!" Don't end up "over the handlebars" because right now things seem scary and more than you can handle. I promise that you can handle whatever is in front of you. Look where you want to go, look at who you want to become as a returned sister missionary, and then take the steps you need to right now to eventually become that person. For example, if you want to one day have a college degree, then save money, enroll in classes, and prepare yourself to earn that degree. If you eventually want to be married in the temple, put yourself in situations to get to know worthy priesthood holders who will be able to take you to the temple, and make yourself the type of person who would be easy to be married to. If you want to be a mother one day, learn to cook, clean, study the scriptures, and to be kind and loving to the people you are close to right now. Don't look down at who you are right now and get discouraged or focus on the obstacles. You will encounter bumps every single day, so being successful will require you to consistently look forward to your next goal. Take the steps to make your life about the things that will make you who you want to be in the future.

> "I believe the devil works even harder when we are home to have us doubt our faith. He doesn't want us to have an eternal family. He wants our faith and the gospel to stop with our generation. If we do slip up, he wants us to forget about the plan of salvation and to feel like there is no repentance for us. Despair is always from the devil." —Anonymous

The world needs talented, strong women with a deep understanding of God's plan for His children. Thankfully, sister, *you* are just that! Precisely because of the strength and ability you gained on your mission, Satan is going to work hard at tearing you down. In this chapter we are going to discuss four challenges that might become obstacles as we come home and look toward the future. All are subtle but all will cause a capable rock star RSM to "look down" and possibly hit the dirt.

1. Feeling Left Behind

In the first few months of my mission, my grandpa passed away. I had always felt really close to him, and he was so supportive of my decision to serve a mission. When I went to visit my grandmother after returning home from my mission, I would always expect to see Grandpa. I hadn't been home when he was sick or for his passing and his funeral, so in many ways it felt like it hadn't really happened. Life keeps moving while we are serving a mission, and although we are not there to be a part of it, we must eventually come home and face the changes. It is easy to feel a little misplaced in all of the newness when arriving home. This sister had a similar experience:

> "It was very hard for me to come back home after my mission. I was dedicated and really worked to give everything I had. When I got home, I felt a little lost because I had no job, I missed school enrollment deadlines, I left my mission family and friends, and my old friends had moved on with their lives. The inherent difficulties involved in coming home don't necessarily mean you are having an identity crisis. Transition is hard, but our identities shouldn't change because we have the best anchor for our identities: the gospel." —Anonymous

Often returned missionaries feel like they have been forgotten by God when returning home because their life at home is drastically different. We move fast in the LDS culture, don't we? Someone is always getting married or having a baby; it is hard to keep track! When I entered the MTC, I thought it would be fun to keep all of the wedding invitations from roommates and close friends sent to me while I was serving. After being out just three months, my collection had reached over ten invitations. I quickly realized I wouldn't have space to keep everything together. This sister found the same thing:

> "By the time I got home from my mission, most of my friends had either gotten married or graduated from BYU and moved away. It was a big adjustment to make new friends and start over, but everything worked out great eventually." —Anonymous

When coming home from a mission, you might feel a little left behind. Although others might have progressed in different ways, this doesn't mean you were left behind. In fact, if you stop and look at those you were close to, you will probably see how much the Lord has blessed their lives while you were gone.

When I left on my mission, my sister was going through an extremely difficult time in her life. It was almost unbearable for me to say good-bye when I knew she was experiencing such pain, but I knew that serving a mission was the right thing to do. During my mission I prayed for her, fasted for her almost every week, and wrote her often. When I returned, she had graduated from college and had a darling, caring, righteous boyfriend; a great job; and great friends. She seemed sincerely happy for the first time in years. She told me the first week I was home that her boyfriend would be coming to my homecoming. And guess what? I was so mad! Ticked! I couldn't believe she wanted to spend time with him and not me—what had happened to my bestie? I look back now and recognize how selfish I was acting. God had answered my prayers! Do you remember in Doctrine and Covenants 100:1 when the Lord talks to Joseph and Sidney? They had been away from their families and were concerned for them, and this is what the Lord tells them: "Your families are well; they are in mine hands, and I will do with them as seemeth me good; for in me there is all power." The Lord took care of our families (I include friends in this as well) while we were away, and so when we get home we can't be mad that their lives have moved forward. We can only be happy and recognize that our service blessed the lives of those we love most.

And one more thing, sister. When you start to feel overwhelmed with how others' lives have changed or feel left behind, it is important to recognize how much *you* have changed in the last eighteen months. You have grown more, learned more, and had more opportunity to feel the love of the Lord than you probably have ever had up to this point of your life. You should feel stoked about who you are and how you have blossomed! Think about how many scriptures, hymns, and types of people you have come to know. Think about the geographic area you were able to see and the opportunities you had to learn to speak in public, teach, and listen. You were given eighteen months of life lessons on steroids! If anything, sisters who were not able to serve a mission are looking at you and feeling envious of your opportunity to become such a rock star sister. Every time you start to feel left behind or overwhelmed by the changes around you—stop. Think of one thing the Lord has given you in the past few years. Be sensitive and appreciative of what you have been able to do.

2. Facing Insecurity

> "[After returning home] I struggled with feeling I had not been a good missionary. In speaking with former sisters and elders from my mission, I constantly compared my mission to theirs. I had low numbers, I didn't teach a lot, and my Polish wasn't as good as theirs was, so naturally in my mind they must have been better missionaries than I was. They must have had more faith, had the Lord's help more abundantly, and worked harder than I had. It wasn't until about two years after I got home, and after a year of professional counseling and a spiritual epiphany, that I finally came to terms with the fact that the work I did on my mission was good and was accepted by the Lord. It wasn't easy, but now I can look back on my mission and who I was on my mission happily and fondly, and I can say that I loved my mission."
> —Sister Lauren R.

It is important that we work hard on not letting insecurity creep into our lives. When we are new at something or in an uncomfortable environment, it is too easy to let insecure thoughts control our thought process. Destructive thoughts like these need to be nipped as soon as they start. Lock your heart to these feelings! I am serious! In fact, I have never been more serious. *Do not* allow any feeling of insecurity or self-doubt to dwell in your heart or mind. I find it helpful to have something that I do physically when something enters my mind that in any way makes me feel less than I am. Elder Boyd K. Packer gave this idea in a 2003 CES Devotional:

> "I gave a talk once in which I likened the mind to a stage. There is always something going on in that stage. Whatever you think is going on in the stage, these ideas and promptings and temptations will move in from the side. What do you do about it? You ought to have a delete key.
>
> "I know a little about computers because my grandchildren have taught me. I know that every computer keyboard has a delete key. If there is something there

you do not want, something you did that you want to get rid of, you underline it and delete it.

"You can have a delete key in your mind. Your mind is in charge, and your body is the instrument of your mind. Now you will have to figure out a delete key for yourself.

"One man showed me once that he used his wedding ring. He said that whenever there was an unworthy thought that tried to get into his mind—and those influences are everywhere—he just rubbed his thumb against his wedding ring. That was the delete key, 'Get out of my mind! I am in charge!'

"You are in command. You cannot say that you do not know any better. You do know better!"[13]

Here are some common insecurities that might enter our "stage." It is helpful to identify them so we can quickly expel them from our mind.

+ I was not a good missionary.

+ I did not do enough as a missionary.

+ The Lord is not pleased with who I am.

+ I am not capable of graduating, getting a job, or making new friends.

+ I am awkward.

+ I am totally alone; I am the only one who is still a single returned sister missionary.

+ I look fat, ugly, and out of style.

+ I will never get married.

+ Everyone has moved forward; I have been left behind.

+ People must think poorly of me.

How depressing is that list? I felt awful just typing out the words! What is scary is how often we harbor those thoughts, allow them to stay in our minds, and even believe them as truth.

Remember how good you felt when you opened your mission call? Or the first time you watched an investigator pray? Or how great you feel when you go for a hike, get together with an old friend, or talk to your mom on the phone after a long day? Think about those feelings and remember, *that* is how the Lord wants you to feel. Those feelings of warmth, love, and confidence are what He wants for His children.

The Lord wants us to be happy and to feel joy, but the adversary will try to undermine that. "[The devil] persuadeth no man to do good, no, not one; neither do his angels; neither do they who subject themselves unto him" (Moroni 7:17). Elder Boyd K. Packer refers to these two patterns that will try to influence us as "conflicting patterns."

You will have just what you want. On one hand, you have inspiration from the Holy Ghost, and, on the other hand, you have what President Ezra Taft Benson called "sinspiration" from the angels of the devil. They are with you all of the time.

So you are the focus of two conflicting patterns trying to influence you in your life, trying to have you go this way or that way (see Matthew 6:24; Luke 16:13; James 1:8). You are the one who makes the decision.

As the old man a generation ago said, "The Lord's votin' for me, and the devil's votin' against me, but it's my vote that counts!" And that is good, solid doctrine.

If you have allowed yourself to let feelings of insecurity find a home in your mind and heart, ask the Lord to help you get rid of them. Pray sincerely to find a way to keep yourself from buying into these doubts. This is a pivotal time in your life, and you need to feel God's love as strongly as possible. Finding your future will require you to feel the Lord's love. Also, there are people who need your love, and when you walk around with a burden of insecurity, it will hinder your ability to demonstrate the affection and kindness you are capable of showing.

Is it easy to get rid of insecurity? No. It is extremely difficult. I will forever be working on not allowing feelings of insecurity to creep into my mind. Use your delete key, prayer, and scripture study, and surround yourself with positive people. Do whatever it takes to nix the insecurities in your life. You do not deserve to carry that burden.

3. Dealing with Depression, Anxiety, or Emotional Instability

A few years after my mission, I felt lower than I had ever felt. I began to visit with a counselor. I had never met with a counselor and had never dealt with an emotional illness. It took me a long time to make the decision to go see someone; I feared what people would think of me if they found out I had to visit a professional for emotional help. One day, while I was hiding my face in the waiting room of the BYU Counseling Center, I saw a friend of mine. She had served a mission just before I did, and I had always really looked up to her. I thought, "She is so on top of everything in her life; there is no way *she* is visiting with a counselor." She didn't see me, but I will always remember how surprised I was to see her. I was sure I was the only one who ever cried, felt out of control, or needed to reach out for help. Now I look back and recognize that the reason she is on top of everything is *because* she is the type of woman who was brave enough to reach out for help when she needed it.

You Are NOT ALONE

Many sisters shared stories of dealing with depression after returning from their missions. Here are a few:

"I went through a small depression right after my mission, and it took a lot of prayer and family help to straighten out my thoughts and feelings. I went on dates and was comfortable, but it still was a lot of work to create good friends. The Spirit really did help me in that department. The thing that helped me the most was knowing that God still loved me and wouldn't leave me. I was still His daughter." —Anonymous

"I returned early from my mission due to severe depression. Because of this, I struggled to feel the Spirit and function in general for quite a while. However, the Atonement, friends and family, a little medication, and time helped me heal, and today I regularly enjoy the Spirit. I have been home for almost two years and am now married. My testimony was greatly strengthened by going through this trial. It was certainly the hardest thing I have yet experienced. Healing from it allowed me to feel the saving and enabling power of the Atonement deeper than ever before in my life. I know the Savior knows us and our struggles and pains, whatever they are. He healed me and will do the same for you, because He and our Heavenly Father love you and know that you can overcome." —Sister Diane E.

"The first few years after I got back, my testimony was quite strong. I've been back for five years now, and in the last year or so my testimony has struggled more. I've dealt with some emotional illness, which makes it difficult to discern between my own feelings and the promptings of the Spirit." —Anonymous

Those who ignore or push away emotional instability will find that it manifests itself later in life. It can be taxing on your relationships with others and God. I see trouble with pushing away an emotional illness for three reasons:

It destroys the way you think about yourself.
It clouds your communication with the Spirit.
It harms your relationship with others.

It is natural to second-guess yourself or feel embarrassed about reaching out for help. Often in the Church we think, "If I just pray and work hard enough, I can make everything better." This is true, to a degree. But the reason the Lord has blessed us with medical professionals and prescription medicine is to help us be happy. Remember how that is our ultimate goal? "Adam fell that men might be; and men are, that they might have *joy* [!]" (2 Nephi 2:25; emphasis added). Walking around with the burden of a emotional illness can seriously distract our hearts and minds from the goodness in the world and, if not addressed, may leave us with deep emotional scars. Please do not allow this to happen to you. Reaching out for help does not mean that you will need to take medicine or have to be diagnosed permanently with an emotional disorder. It just means that you care about your happiness and the happiness of the people around you enough to understand when you need help. Do not let your pride keep you from receiving care for something the Lord would not want you to pass through alone.

4. Experiencing an Identity Crisis

"Before my mission, I was 'Cherise.' During my mission, I was 'Hermana C.' When I came home, I didn't want to just be Cherise anymore; I had learned so much. I also didn't want to be Hermana C. anymore. I had the quest to find out who I was as 'Cherise C.' It wasn't easy because I was starting at step 1 in finding myself, but eventually I was at step 2, and then step 3, and then eventually I realized—wow, I know who I am again. Be patient." —Sister Cherise C.

This was my question as a returned sister missionary: How am I supposed to come home and be "myself" when I don't even know who I am? Coming home and not knowing who I was stood as the greatest challenge in my return home from a mission. I still understood my eternal identity, but I had lost all of the short-term characteristics that had once made me "me." My crisis was completely validated when I interviewed more than two hundred sisters for this book. They had also faced similar battles in the daily quest to "find themselves."

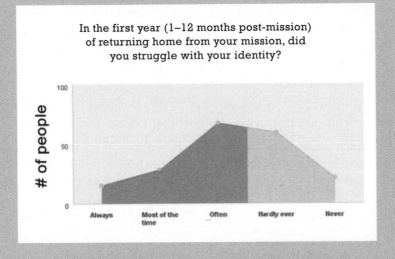

You Are NOT ALONE

Of the over two hundred sisters surveyed, nearly 60 percent felt like they "always," "most of the time," or "often" struggled with their identity in the first year of returning from their missions.

In the first year (1–12 months post-mission) of returning home from your mission, did you struggle with your identity?

# of people

100

50

0

Always | Most of the time | Often | Hardly ever | Never

One sister said this:

"It's been hard for me to define who I am like I used to before the mission. Before I left, I had a very clear and defined sense of self—what I liked and disliked, what role I played in social situations, what style of clothes I wore, what music I listened to, what colors I wanted my house to be decorated in, and what I did in my free time. A lot of these aspects of myself changed (or rather disappeared) while I was on my mission. Although they are seemingly trivial things in comparison to the grander and more important aspects of self that identify us—such as being daughters of God—I find myself less confident in social situations because I am unsure of the things that make me 'me.' It's kind of like feeling like a pre-teen again." —Anonymous

Sister, you nailed it! That is *exactly* how I felt when I returned. It was a process to remember what I loved and what made me happy. I spent so much time psychoanalyzing myself, it was absurd. It bugged me to think I had lost "me." But sis, I wasn't lost. I had just evolved into a new rad returned sister missionary version of me that I didn't even know existed.

After I married, graduated from college, and then later became a mom, I realized that this process of finding my groove and figuring out who I was in my new role happened with each life change. When I came home from my mission, I spent so much time worrying that I was lost that I didn't even get to enjoy what an awesome version of me I had become. I remember my little brother saying to me one day, "You're so nice!" I was taken back; he actually liked this new, weird, returned sister missionary me? I guess I wasn't as bad as I thought.

So, I guess what I'm trying to say is—enjoy the new you. It is probably a really good you. Sure you might not know any of the hip bands, and you might be a little out of touch when it comes to the happening social scene, but you are pretty great because you just got home from serving the Lord, and you did a really great job while you were there.

Don't Stop Reading Here!

These four stumbling blocks can be tough. I have felt left behind, am constantly trying to ward off insecurity, have experienced forms of emotional illness, and am constantly reworking my identity. You might think I am a total disaster by this point, but I just consider myself normal. Sister, you know I would never leave you hanging. If any of the above-mentioned challenges resonates with you, I hope you will keep reading because I have a solution for you. In the next chapter I give you my three life-changing steps to finding your future. It's going to be so good!

Chapter Eleven

THREE STEPS TO FINDING YOUR FUTURE

> "Forget yourself. Just go for it. Do the things you love. Love others. Look to lift and serve. Continue to invite people to come unto Christ. Get to know people. Be bold. Smile. Have fun. Don't hold anything back. Take things one day, or one week, at a time. Remember your experiences and the principles you have been teaching for the past year and a half. Be exactly obedient. Relax. The transition home is hard for everyone. It takes time. Hold to the rod, have faith in the Savior, and be patient! Life is wonderful; enjoy it." —Sister Marielle N.

IN THE LAST CHAPTER, WE ESTABLISHED SOME STUMbling blocks. Now let's talk about how we move past these obstacles and find our future. It will only take three steps! It is just that easy. I know I am sounding a little like an infomercial, but I mean it. Continue reading to learn how easily you can find your future as a returned sister missionary.

1. Decide Who You Want to Be

Sometimes I can't remember what really makes me happy, what I really want to accomplish in life, and what I'm working toward. So this is what I do . . . are you ready? I imagine my funeral. Gruesome, right? Just hang with me. I think, "What would I want people to say about me at my funeral? Who would I want there? What do I want it to feel like?" Asking these questions reminds me what I really value, because when all is said and done, I value some things more than others and those are the things that make me *me*. And what makes me *me* is where I should be spending my time every day; it is how I am able to be myself.

So now you want to know what my funeral will be like, don't you? (Or what I hope it will be like . . . And yes, you are *totally* invited.) This whole "live like you want your funeral to be like" idea came to me after attending my great Aunt Leola Green Merrill's funeral while I was a sophomore in college. She had four kids, and they all had a million children who were darling, well dressed, educated, and well spoken. At Leola's funeral, the stake center was packed with people who loved Leola and remembered her for her outspoken wit and dedication to the gospel. They remembered the loving things she did and said, such as how she would call every person in the ward when they received a new calling to tell them how great they would be. Darling, right? Why don't I do that? Or how she would invite the Primary kids over to rehearse their talks. People also mentioned things like what a fabulous public speaker she was and how in love she and her husband were.

I decided right then that I wanted a funeral just like Leola's, and so I had better start living in a way that would help me be the type of person who leaves a legacy like the one of my Aunt Leola. So when I feel like "I don't even know who I am!" I think of my funeral, and I think, "Am I a woman who reaches out to my local ward on a level that is meaningful to them? Am I preparing myself to have children? Do I spend time developing my talents?" Then those are the things that I work on every day because that is what I want to be—that is who I want to become. And whether or not we are who we want to eventually be, with the Lord on our side we will one day be there. Here are two other strategies that sisters used in the search to find themselves after a mission:

> "I had to learn how to stay true to what I felt was the "real" me that I had found as a missionary, but also to maintain and be that me in real life. It took me a while to do so consistently. I really felt like I was still growing up." —Anonymous

> "[I made the transition] by speaking often with the Lord about my identity and what He thinks of me and by not being too hard on myself for not being perfect. I needed to learn to chill out, and then I felt more successful." —Anonymous

So, sis, think about who you want to be. That is what you need to do every day to be yourself, to be the best you.

2. Set Goals

> "I didn't struggle with my identity as much as I struggled to know what I wanted to get out of life. You see, I didn't set goals or make plans for after my mission, so I was starting from scratch. Goals and dreams make a world of difference. They are what has given me the freedom to feel like I can just be myself. Plans can change; the important thing is to do your own thing, guided by the Spirit and following what you truly desire to do in your heart. That way you will have joy in the journey." —Sister Rose K.

Now that we know who we want to be when all is said and done, let's make it happen! At the end of many chapters in this book, I have included self-analysis quizzes as well as journal prompt questions to help you apply the content directly to your life. Use these sections to help you set goals that apply to your life right now. One of my very favorite quotes is in chapter 8 of *Preach My Gospel*. It says:

> "Goals reflect the desires of our hearts and our vision of what we can accomplish. Through goals and plans, our hopes are transformed into action. Goal setting and planning are acts of faith. Prayerfully set goals that are in harmony with the Savior's command to 'teach all nations, baptizing them in the name of the Father, and of the Son, and of the Holy Ghost' (Matthew 28:19)."[14]

Acts of faith, desires of our hearts, hopes are transformed into action? This is gooooood stuff! Here's what Kelsie had to say about setting goals after a mission:

> "Setting goals helped. I wanted to make sure I was anxiously engaged, whether that was in school, my ward, my family, or my social life. Doing things that are productive for my life and the lives of those around me gave me great satisfaction. Living the lifestyle of a full-time missionary obviously isn't possible, but we can still use our time wisely." —Sister Kelsie E.

The truth! I hope at the conclusion of this book you will take the journal prompts as a way to set goals for the different areas of your life. Use short- and long-term goals to help you work toward who you want to ultimately become. Take the goals seriously and go back occasionally to see what progress you're making. Don't get all crazy or anything, but do use goals as a way to help you get out of life what you really hope to achieve.

Lisa Ward SUPERSTAR

I met Lisa Ruefenacht Ward as a freshman at BYU. Like any good San Francisco native, Lisa has flawless taste in music, short haircuts, and vintage clothing. She is beautiful, smart, and creative, and I have always known she is way cooler than I am. I was especially impressed with Lisa as she transitioned home from her mission to St. Louis, Missouri. She seemed to hold onto the good from her service and not leave it behind when she settled back into civilian life. For those of you who have attempted this, it isn't easy, and I'm excited to share with you what she has to say about this process.

Q *Lisa, let's just say it like it is: You are totally hip and cool. How did you come home from your mission and maintain the spirit of being a returned sister missionary but still feel like you were able to be yourself?*

A Transitioning back into a "normal" person but staying true to the Spirit was the hardest part of coming home. Before my mission, one could rarely find me without at least one earbud in my ear, jamming to some tunes. Fast forward eighteen months— I took two full weeks after being released to finally listen to non-Church music. One thing I remember so clearly from my MTC teacher, Brother Iverson, was him saying that I didn't have to, and shouldn't, come home and be the same person I was before. Change was okay. Change was good. We go on missions in part to find our spirits and draw out that most pure and true version of ourselves. I knew that was what I wanted and needed to do. I wanted to come home a better person, and more important, I wanted to stay that way.

It took me a long time to reconcile who I was then with who I had become. This "new me" wasn't as interested in collecting vinyl or playing in rock bands. I was able to frequently attend the temple when I came home, which helped ease the transition. I spent time exploring new interests and trying new things. On missions we learn how to effectively set and achieve goals, so I implemented those skills. Three and a half years later, I think I'm a pretty balanced version of my old self and my mission self.

The point is: Don't come home and try to be who you were before your mission, because you're not that person anymore. As missionaries we strip away worldly interests and are left with our truest selves. Embrace your divine self. Spend time trying new things and exploring your true interests. Eventually you will find that happy medium and be able to reconcile your spiritual self with worldly pursuits. If I can drive one thing home above all others, continue to define yourself by spiritual means, not worldly means. Be a daughter of a loving God first and foremost, and always conduct yourself in accordance with being a disciple of Christ. In my experience, everything else falls naturally in line when those are our top priorities.

Q *Love this. Well said. During this process, how did you keep the Spirit in your life?*

A This was, and still is, one of the hardest aspects of coming home. Before my mission and while growing up, I never had good personal or family scripture study habits. Admittedly, I still don't. But there are two absolutes I never slip up on. First, daily meaningful prayer. It's not always on my knees where it should be, but my Father in Heaven loves me more than anyone, and He deserves a good conversation with me. One habit of prayer I formed as a sister missionary was that of praying for others before myself. It's so easy to get caught up in what we need. Prayer is so much more powerful when we pray for others first. My faith is strengthened by praying for others and seeing how Heavenly Father uses me to bless them. This also leads into my second absolute, which is service. I reflect daily (yes, even still, several years after coming home) on the people I taught on my mission. I still talk to many of them weekly—at least monthly. Maintaining relationships with them feeds my desire to serve my fellow brothers and sisters and share our Father's love with them as I did as a missionary. We may not be called as missionaries, but the first great commandments are to love God, then love others. Keeping these as priorities has kept me focused on creating eternal relationships, connections that anchor me amid all the day-to-day craziness we inevitably sink back into.

Q *Lisa, you are a dream returned sister missionary. Do you have any more advice to share with other returned sister missionaries?*

A Be your best self. You have all these skills now that you probably didn't have before, so use them. Don't let your desires consume you to the point that you forget what is most important. Things will unfold in the Lord's time. They always do. He loves you. He has not forgotten you. He will bless you now just as He blessed you and those you taught as a missionary. Let things happen as they are supposed to. Love others, and let that love guide you to good opportunities and good people. Also, feed the missionaries. Be the member missionary you needed when you were a missionary.

Tell Me about It, SISTER

"Before I served a mission, I thought I knew who I was. I was Crys Kevan, a smart, strong, independent woman, who liked to play soccer, read, travel, and learn about new cultures and places. But then I became Sister Kevan as a missionary, and I struggled to find out who she was. What does it mean when they say to 'lose yourself in the work'? I struggled to understand what that meant. Soon I realized that it means you stop focusing on yourself all the time and you serve the Lord with all your heart. It means you try to be exactly obedient, but put love above all. It means you care about your companion when she needs you. It means sometimes you stay up late talking to your companion even though that is against the rules. It means you spend as much time as you can thinking about your investigators, less-active members, and other ward members—not for the sake of 'being a good missionary' but because you love them and want to be a great tool in the hands of God. That is how Crys Kevan became Sister Kevan.

"But making the transition back wasn't as easy. I felt I had changed. I was still strong, smart, and independent, but I couldn't remember what I was interested in. I found it difficult to relate to what others were talking about for the first week. I thought I needed to reconstruct Crys Kevan from Sister Kevan, but then I realized that who I really am never changed at all. As a missionary I was loving and strong and independent, but I still worked with my companion. I was still interested in other cultures on my mission; I still had goals to go on to graduate school and travel the world. All of me was still there, it just took me a few months to realize that Sister Kevan and Crys Kevan are the same person. I just adapted to the calling and let the Lord use me as me. It took me a while to find my grounding, and sure, I was awkward and didn't want to touch boys, let alone hug them. I had to force myself to go on dates and do things other than read

Preach My Gospel. But ultimately it doesn't matter, because wherever I am and whatever I do, I am me."
—Sister Crys K.

3. Keep Going

Recently I was having a really hard day. I had been so happy, things were moving along so well in life, and then all of a sudden, it was as if in one day everything came crashing down around me. As I was going to bed that night, unbelievably discouraged, I made a list of all of the things that I was worried about, all of the questions I had about my life that was feeling like a total disaster. I then read my scriptures looking for answers (like I suggest you do in chapter 7!) and found some comfort, but not the big "This is it!" answer I was in search of. I got on my knees to pray, and that is when it came! Are you ready? Here's what it was: "Keep going." The Spirit told me to "keep going." I was looking for a solution to all of these problems, and what Heavenly Father told me was to just keep going. I took this to mean that my solution would come if I would just pull myself together and press through the hard days and nights I was facing. And so, sis, I am going to say the same thing to you today. Keep going! The third step to finding your future will be to push through some hard days, weeks, months, maybe even years, and look where you want to go.

The more I think about this "keep going" idea, the more I realize that I'm not the first person who was given this instruction. In Lehi's vision of the tree of life, the people holding to the rod signify those who were moving toward Christ, "and they did press forward through the mist of darkness" (1 Nephi 8:24). And the hymn "Press Forward Saints" is a total call to keep moving forward. But I think my favorite words about pressing forward come from 2 Nephi 31:20:

> "Wherefore, ye must press forward with a steadfastness in Christ, having a perfect brightness of hope, and a love of God and of all men. Wherefore, if ye shall press forward, feasting upon the word of Christ, and endure to the end, behold, thus saith the Father: Ye shall have eternal life."

Sister, Nephi is right! If you can just move forward, you will get through any rough patches and find your future. Maybe moving forward right now means that you are just barely holding onto the rod, maybe it means that you are tackling challenges and goals. Pressing forward will always mean that we are looking toward the Savior. We are all doing this together! I hope you are encouraged to keep going, keep fighting, keep praying, and to spend some time meditating on how to be the best returned sister missionary possible. Then work, work, work like you never stopped being a missionary. This third step in finding your future will probably be the most challenging because it will require patience and faith. You might feel a little out of control at times, but as we have heard from countless sisters in this book, one day you will wake up and think, "Oh, this is me, here I am! I feel so normal, confident, and comfortable. And I am so, so pretty too!" Until that day, you might have some moments feeling like a fish out of water, trying to make your way onto the right path. While you are coming down the mountain, just make sure you sit back and look where you want to go. It takes time to do hard things, and uniting our missions with our home lives is hard. It is the right thing to do and that is what makes it a challenge. Don't give up, sister; you are doing great!

Self-Analysis Quiz

Response Key

    1 = never   4 = almost always

    2 = sometimes   5 = always

    3 = often

Please use the key to honestly answer these statements:

_____ I allow insecurity to control my thoughts and actions.

_____ I feel depressed and anxious or deal with emotional instability on a daily basis.

_____ I often compare myself to others.

_____ I choose activities daily based on the joy they bring me.

_____ I look forward to the future and set goals to become someone great.

Journal Prompts

What strengths has Heavenly Father blessed me with? What are my short-term goals? What are my long-term goals? What am I doing right now to accomplish these goals? What insecure thoughts can I work on deleting from my mind? What positive thoughts will I replace the negative ones with?

_____

_____

_____

_____

_____

_____

_____

_____

_____

_____

_____

_____

_____

_____

_____

_____

_____

_____

_____

_____

_____

_____

_____

_____

_____

_____

_____

_____

_____

_____

_____

_____

_____

_____

_____

_____

_____

_____

_____

Conclusion

DOES IT HAVE TO END?

"Perspective is everything. Missions are awesome, but we have to remember that a missionary's life is somewhat a sheltered existence, only focusing on gospel topics, being assigned a person to work and live with, and not worrying about finding a job or being accepted socially. Life will always have its high points and low points. Dating is always awkward. Everyone faces some degree of identity crisis. However, mission experiences strengthen you to withstand what life throws at you. You learn what it takes to be with someone 24-7. You learn to study, to work, to be disciplined, and to be a disciple. You learn where true joy comes from, and you grow in your capacity to serve in the Church and in your family. Our attitude should be to treasure missionary experiences, not pine away for them." —Sister Emily S.

ECAUSE SISTER MISSIONARIES ARE NOT EXPECTED to serve missions, I think that sometimes when we do serve we expect to come home and have blessings that other females don't. We might imagine these blessings to be things like attractive male returned missionaries who sweep us off our feet, financial security, or acceptance into a top university. Although these are all wonderful blessings, we should not expect that these things will just happen to returned missionaries automatically. Remember when you made the decision to serve a mission? It was not because you were more righteous than another female or deserving of more blessings. It was because you had "the desire" to serve and those are they who are "called to the work" (Doctrine and Covenants 4:3).

My Reward

So what are the blessings or rewards from serving a mission? What do we have to look forward to? The reward from serving a mission came the day you opened your call! Or maybe even the day you prayed and received an answer to serve. The rewards are the experiences we have while serving that we will always have with us—the experiences that soften our hearts, deepen our faith, and teach us a pattern of relying on Christ for all things. The rewards are the opportunities to see the gospel in action in the lives of those we taught and the eternal knowledge and truths we were able to see take hold of people's lives and in our own. These are the real blessings, and these experiences will allow us to come home and continue to build our relationship with the Savior.

What I'm suggesting is that everything might not happen to us that we had pictured when we first came home. What we will have is a deep understanding of the Atonement and the ability to find peace through whatever may come. The best blessing of all, right? Right.

Okay, I Promise This Is It

I love you, sister! I really do. I love your choice to serve a mission. I love your choice to read a book about coming home and being better. One day I hope we can get together over a Diet Coke and talk about your favorite section in *Preach My Gospel*, who you are dating, and your best tracting stories. That sounds so wonderful. Until then, continue to pray, read your scriptures, and spend some quiet time every single day listening for the Spirit.

It is a blessing to be a woman; to be blessed with the ability to love, nurture, and care for others in a unique way. It is a blessing to be a sister missionary; to have the joy of serving and teaching others the gospel of Jesus Christ. God loves you and is so amazed by the decisions you make to be good and to love those around you. The news of Jesus Christ you shared while serving a mission is true. He died for us and lives again. He knows you, your joys, and your sorrows during this time in your life. Cling to the Savior and His teachings. He will take care of you, I promise you.

Thank you for spending this time with me. I hope you will join me on the "Tell Me about It, Sister!" Facebook page and unite with an army of returned sister missionaries who are ready to help, inspire, and lift one another.

Loving you, sis,

Xo

Andrea

Remember This:

- God loves you.
- You were a great missionary; God is pleased with your service.
- Give yourself time to adjust from your mission.
- You are beautiful—a total babe!
- Work hard at whatever you do.
- In order to get married, you first have to date.
- Be the welcome wagon.
- Rock those skinny jeans.
- Don't miss a month as a visiting teacher.
- Live the principles you taught others as a missionary.
- The Spirit still guides your life.
- Never miss a day in the scriptures.
- Be the ward member the missionaries can count on.
- Don't harbor insecure thoughts.
- Decide who you want to be and set goals to get there.
- Your mission was the beginning of the great things *your* life has in store for you.

ENDNOTES

1. *Preach My Gospel*, 137.

2. Joseph Walker, "LDS Church tweaks dress and grooming requirements for missionaries," *Deseret News*, July 12, 2013.

3. LDS Young Women Theme

4. Earl C. Tingey, "The Simple Truths from Heaven: The Lord's Pattern," CES Fireside, Jan. 13, 2008.

5. Gordon B. Hinckley, "A Conversation with Single Adults," *Ensign*, Mar. 1997.

6. Ibid.

7. M. Catherine Thomas, *Light in the Wilderness: Explorations in the Spiritual Life*, Salt Lake City: Digital Legend, 2010, 102.

8. Jeffrey R. Holland, "Lord, I Believe," *Ensign*, May 2013.

9. Neil L. Andersen, "It's a Miracle," *Liahona*, May 2013.

10. *Preach My Gospel*, 156.

11. Ibid., 214.

12. Ibid.

13. Ibid., 146.

14. Ibid.

ABOUT THE AUTHOR

ANDREA FAULKNER WILLIAMS IS A WRITER, MARketer, wife, mother, and returned sister missionary. She served in the Illinois Nauvoo Mission as well as the Colorado Colorado Springs Mission. A graduate of Brigham Young University with a BA in Latin American Studies, she currently runs her own company selling all-natural children's bath products, Tubby Todd Bath Co. She and her husband, Brian, live in San Diego with their two babes, Josie Jean and Walker Todd. Connect with her and hundreds of other RSMs at www.tellmeaboutitsister.com.

Acknowledgments

A special "thank you," "I love you," and "I could not have done it without you!" goes to:

The "Superstar Sisters" interviewed for the book: Christin, Jamie, Brittany, Erin, Melanie, Jessica, and Lisa.

The two editors: Marilyn Green Faulkner (Japan Sendi Mission) and Sarah Gibby Perris (England London Mission).

Last, I would like to thank and recognize the over two hundred returned sister missionaries who contributed to this book through their participation in a survey sent to them in July 2011. Their responses form the heart and soul of this book.